You not
w[...]
Don't sell yourself
Short. ♡

An Everyday Mama Finds a Passionate Life

By Olga Pyshnyak-Lawrence

To the everyday mama that is willing to find a passionate life

Table of Contents

Introduction

Here is a disclaimer. I was not raised in an optimistic, life is peachy home. I was not told that life is a bed of roses. Nor was I told that life is a box of chocolates, you never know what you are going to get. I knew exactly what was expected of me: a mediocre, grey, unfulfilling existence. Something no one wanted for themselves but kept handing over to their children. An inheritance of burdens.

Growing up in a Slavic, super religious home meant to me that I was expected to become like my mother. A second-class citizen in her own home, subservient, lonely, misunderstood and devoid of hobbies.

Let me explain.

My father was the ultimate boss, the most authoritarian figure you can imagine. He believed that he could even make us think the way he thought. As if he could get into our heads and implant those thoughts deep within our psyche until his thoughts were our homegrown thoughts.

He used to say, "If you don't know how to do it, I will teach you. If you don't want to do it, I will make you."

He misused the Bible like so many countless religious men who always failed to figure out why their wives seemed so lackluster. Here's the reason why; because a woman thrives under a constant watering of love. You cannot love someone you deride and find consistently beneath you.

Nor can someone feel loved while they feel like a slave tied to a pole of meager existence.

Sure, the women tried. They did. But it wasn't their fault, or perhaps it was, because they never banded together to stand up for

1

what was rightfully theirs. For the men to love them in the way that Christ requested. To give up themselves for their wives. To be willing to lay down their lives.

Anyway, there was my future. A husband like that? Forget it. I rebelled.

Another huge issue I've noticed in our communities, which was not considered a problem, but carried as a badge of honor, that sense of martyrdom with which women measured themselves and others around them. Who had the least time to themselves? Who wasn't "lazy"? Who didn't have time to do anything besides looking after her husband, children, and home?

If you were like my mom, she didn't even have time to slap on some cream on her face. I know. I've bought her some, a few times, after which I stopped. She never used them.

Most women in my community have many children. I am the oldest of eight. Most of my childhood years were spent babysitting. I've babysat my sister when I was five and she was almost three. Our parents went to work and we stayed home.

Of course, that was another time and in another culture.

So before I digress, I want you to know that I am not bitter. I am very proud of my roots and my parents did the best they could in an unknown country, with plenty of sacrifices under their belt. Sometimes they exercised control in their life in the best way they could.

Suffice it to say, I rebelled against my future, my culture and my parents' expectations, not because I wanted to do this, spurred on by any form of teenage angst, no. I just didn't see myself fitting into that box. It wasn't true to me.

Why am I telling you this? Because what I am about to share with you in the next few chapters didn't come easily to me. I wasn't taught this. No one exemplified these principles to me.

If I can live passionately, so anyone else can.

If I, who was often told that my thoughts and ideas don't matter, to shut up, hush up, that even God doesn't listen to me, who sacrificed her youth to serve her family and worked since I was twelve (my sister was nine, cleaning dirty offices...) and that was not appreciated but found lacking, in the never-enough kind of way... Please, so can you override your way of thinking to start thinking fresh and through the truth colored glasses. You can do it. I have all the faith in you.

Onto happier pastures!

My peeking out of the cocoon happened around the time of my breaking free from the physical authority of my father. That meant that I no longer lived under his roof. It took me a few more years to get out psychologically.

Because I never conformed to the expectations placed on me: living in the parents' home, getting married, only then, moving out, and having gazillion kids, I realized I might as well start thinking for myself.

I was 24.

Don't get me wrong, I've made some mistakes because now I could make them freely. In the process I did learn what served me and what didn't. What gave my voice clarity and what stifled my expressions.

I finally came out fully, and committed to this journey to discover the secret of passionate living when I gave birth to my most amazing, most beautiful daughter in the whole wide world.

She is the secret of my success. She motivates me, each time I look at her, to leave this world a little bit better, to leave her a legacy she could be proud of and would use to grow from and thrive. My ceiling must be her floor.

I don't want her picking up scraps from my floor.

I must admit, I struggled so much internally with regards to valuing myself as a stay-at-home mom. It was something I looked down upon while growing up. Because my father didn't value my mother, I thought my husband couldn't possibly value me.

I'm no expert, but what I do know is that what we feel, we project on others, we allow them to treat us the way we expect to be treated.

I was tired and lonely, having moved away from my family in Massachusetts all the way to Athens, GA. (Love this city, by the way. Worth a visit!)

Needless to say, my husband and I had to learn to polish the jagged edges of our relationship during this phase of our lives. I had to learn to trust him, that he did indeed value me even though I wasn't part of the corporate world anymore, but was elbow deep in dishes and diapers. He had to learn to appreciate that my home base is now my office and that I am indeed busy and don't have time to waste. That I am not eating bonbons on the comfy sofa, watching day shows, while our child sleeps angelically next to me.

I realized that something was missing from my otherwise happy life. I wasn't completely fulfilled. That something seemed to be passing me by, that I wasn't living fully, that there was something else out there for me and my family.

Once I got over my guilt for not feeling fulfilled at a time which many would expect, giddy on maternal bliss, I began to explore my feelings.

I began my quest to find the secret of living on another level. To finally dream again like a kid. To believe that anything is possible, that the world is truly my oyster. I've believed all those ideals despite my past, but sometime after college, after hitting the "real world" it all passed away like a fine mist. I couldn't hold onto it.

I was driven to find that secret for my child. I didn't want her wasting her life away, believing things that weren't true or disbelieving that God had a wonderful, amazing plan for her life.

I knew that living with passion would set her up for success, for reaching levels many dream of but stop short of, because someone put a damper on that excited flame.

Without further ado, in the midst of wild mommy-hood, here are my secrets to living a passionate life that will take your existence to another level!

Enjoy and thrive, my dear mama!

Let's start from the beginning

It all started at a time when I least expected it to start. It was so unexpected, so welcome, so appreciated but barely understood, that it took me a few months to realize what was happening to me. The events took hold of me in a way that I couldn't recognize because none of this had ever happened to me before. A wave overcame me and I was helpless to protest, all I could do was give in and succumb to the delicious feeling of riding the highest wave of my life. The only way I could stay on this wave was to stop holding on, because I couldn't, but to just let it take care of the pace set before me by God himself.

So, let me start at the beginning.

It was a week before the New Year's Day of 2017, a big year for me as this was going to be the year of my turning 33, a double-digit date of big significance, nearing the year of 35, which would make me half a decade close to 40, 40 being so close to being 50, middle-aged. So, yes, 33 was going to be big but I didn't realize it was going to be THAT BIG.

My sister Pollyanna was visiting (yes, for you classics buffs out there, my mom did indeed name my sister after the fictitious character, Pollyanna, having heard that story on tape while being pregnant).

My husband's brother was visiting for the holidays as well.

Polly had flown in from Massachusetts and Paul, Chris's brother, from Germany, a young girl and an older gentleman, who bonded so well, to the point of Paul gifting my sister with a puppy! My parents were not thrilled to find *that* surprise in Pollyanna's arms at their doorstep.

I always get a bit crazy when we have guests in town. I panic about everything being perfect, but not too perfect, because that would be boring. I don't want to look boring. Some people may prefer a sterile environment, but not me. So, things for me have to look just right.

So, when Chris called me on the way home from picking Paul up at the airport with news of them arriving home much earlier than expected, I wasn't too thrilled. And yes, I told him so. Not because I didn't want to see Paul, but because things were not just so. I wasn't ready to welcome our guest. Unfortunately, I was on the speaker. Paul responded with, "Perhaps I should go back?", after which I was utterly humiliated.

If you haven't noticed, I like to plan, I like to stick to a schedule and to have people think well of me. I am apparently a control freak without realizing it.

I am a type A personality, with a big A. If I didn't get an A in school, I would be near tears.

The details I am throwing at you will become very relevant to my story.

Fast forward a little, we had a fantastic time with our guests, to the best of our ability as a toddler of 16 months was thrown into the mix. We went out a lot. Ate out a lot. Drank some.

Fantastic time. Christmas came and went and then it was that week before New Year's.

Here is when it became very serious. I started to have a small inner voice whisper to me, for Christians, it is easy to recognize this voice as the Holy Spirit, for the non-Christian, the inner you, the voice of the universe, etc. What is relevant to my story is that it spoke to me and told me to write down a list of what I want to see for myself in the next year. I've never done that before. No one showed me how nor ever asked me to.

It was a completely new experience for me. So I said, alright, I will, but let it be an inspired list, may it line up with God's plan.

After having an interesting chat with my sister, we both decided to follow through and write out our plans, goals, desires for the new year, no matter how crazy they seemed, how unreachable, how unapproachable.

We both took out our notebooks and over several evenings proceeded to write out our vision so we may run with it. We took this task very seriously and from now on, based on my incredible results, I will keep doing it every single year.

Oh, and by the way, I made my hubby do it, too.

Even before we welcomed the new year, things started shifting.

It was the day before New Year's Day.

Pollyanna, my daughter Maya and I had a hankering, more like a need, to go to the playground.

The gentlemen followed suit, slightly a little too chipper if you get my drift. A few beers were involved. In Paul's case, a few vodkas perhaps...

I remember exactly where I was when I ran into my acquaintance, a fantastic mom of three, who also managed to run a business full time. I always admired her composure and mommy skills. She seemed to constantly have it together.

Nelly, was everything I wanted to be, or so it seemed.

We had a chat, a mommy chat, where you are always looking everywhere else but the person you are talking to, constantly keeping your eyes on your notoriously flighty child.

Mommy chats used to unnerve me but now I am mostly used to them. You have to learn to never take them personally, as in, if they are still talking to you they probably still want to, otherwise they would make an easy excuse and pretend they have to run after their wild child.

I've mentioned, passionately, how exercise had been such a blessing for me, how it literally saved my sanity during the dark moments, such as when Maya was waking up almost every hour for 11 months straight, days when I lived an hour to hour, when thinking of tomorrow was excruciating. Exercise was a time for me. It no longer was something I had to do. It was something I was so desperate to do! I loved it.

Before we left the playground, Nelly asked me if I was interested in helping her start an exercise program, an extra offering for her current clients. I responded with great interest and went on my merry way, barely believing that she was serious. I was so used to people not following through and saying what they don't mean. Most people want to do something but never get around to step 1. having a plan.

Imagine my surprise when she actually texted me that evening, with considerable interest to take our brainstorming further. I was so pleased for her and for myself! We scheduled to meet up on Monday, the second day of the New Year.

On New Year's Eve, we played Monopoly to stay awake, had a few bottles of wine, ate, chatted, and proceeded to have our butts thoroughly kicked by my little sis, Polly. Never have I seen her competitive side that pronounced as on that night. I think we all were shocked to see the meekness of the lamb be replaced by the roar of a lion.

An hour before the no-return line, Pollyanna and I went upstairs to go over our lists, share them and pray over them. We sensed that something had shifted. The presence of the Spirit was so strong as soon as we began.

After this serious moment, we went downstairs to rejoin the men and continued to celebrate in a not so serious fashion, fireworks. That lasted for a very long time. Sorry, neighbors.

And so it began.

Glory and tribulation

The first Monday of the year found Nelly and I chatting away in a local coffee shop for two hours straight! We were both so lucky to have someone else take care of our children for a change, thanks hubbies!

We were so excited, brimming with ideas. I was excited to be part of a new venture where I could learn a bit about myself as well as share my love of fitness with the world. She was excited to add something new to the clients.

Before going home, we scheduled a consecutive date to meet up and start putting our ideas into action.

I was so happy that I found someone who was excited about following through on her word. She seemed to be serious and brimming with stability. I believed I could rely on her and trust her, otherwise I would not be going ahead with this venture.

The next time we met, we scaled the mountains of brainstorming. We created a survey for the potential interested parties and were both going to send it out to our spheres of influence.

We agreed on the name of our company, Maternal Movement and our moms to be called Motivated Mamas.

Nelly's willing participation seemed to wane right after that.

I didn't notice the signs at the beginning.

I kept plugging away, connecting to the community. Sending out emails and looking up the data we collected from the responses so we could glean the relevant knowledge.

I will give her credit though. She did open up the Facebook accounts, the website and other accounts. I ended up populating them.

Soon, it started to feel like I was pulling teeth, begging her to follow through on her homework, her assignments, her input. Every meeting greeted me with, "Sorry, I didn't do my homework."

The less she seemed to care, the more I seemed to fire up.

One day, I decided that we needed to do something fun. I brought my essential oils over to her shop and said that we should create a perfume for our ladies. We ended up using her oils in our ingredient list and came up with the Motivated Mama Energized roll-on perfume. I was super pumped. My first ever creation for sale!!!

Nelly was going to order the necessary ingredients for us to roll out this invention at her shop. I've never sold anything at a shop before. That small activity taught me that I could create. It felt amazing. And the thought that someone else would enjoy using it, that felt even better.

The ingredients didn't come in for one and a half months or so.

I still carried on, trying to hold onto our relationship. I've designed the logo, the business cards, T-shirts...

And then I got hit with the news that Nelly would no longer have her shop. She was going to focus on her virtual shop and set up pop-up shops around Georgia.

The strategy we had at the outset, to be selling fundraising items for our business and future fitness program, was falling through.

Those news began the cracking in the façade of our partner relationship. What else was she hiding? How could I trust her, especially if she seemed to no longer care, no longer do her work, no longer respond to me... for days? I even had to ask her, months into this venture, to invite her friends to like our page. Did she even care???

It got so bad one day, I had to ask her to send an email in front of me so I would know that chore was done and I could relax.

I hated being the bossy bitch. I hated what I was turning into. Even my tone was turning into a begging speech. I seemed to become apologetic every time I asked her to do the smallest thing.

I started to lose my trust in God. Why would He set me up with someone with whom I just couldn't jibe?

I knew that April would be tough for her. That was the last month of her physical store. I've offered my help and support, trying to be the bigger person. Trying desperately to understand and fit her circumstance into my expectations.

I've brought her coffee to cheer her up one day. I actually told her not to think about doing any work for Maternal Movement during a specific week. To just focus on herself and getting emotionally fit.

That was one of the worst weeks of my life.

That was the week I started resenting her so much. At that point, it was safe to say that I followed through on every promise I've made to her and the company. I even published a book to create awareness and gave it away, hoping to increase the likes on our Facebook page. I've had to add new strategies and alter a course or two because I had no input from her. There was a turning point where I decided to run it all as my own venture and make the decisions I thought would be best. I no longer could wait on her. Any experience I thought I would gain through our association never came through.

Without batting an eye, I could conservatively say that I've done ninety-five percent of the work.

Naturally, I was resentful. Naturally, I would be upset if someone who was supposed to be committed, to what was turning out to be a great passion in my life, appeared to have left us.

Around that time, I've had a meeting with a wise woman, who shined some light onto my plight. She said to me, "Olga, you just gave too much."

That was a lesson I will never forget. In the future, I will have to make sure not to put my heart on a platter when someone is giving me a lollipop.

That week grew with bitterness. My physical heart began to ache each day. My husband was concerned. I had a hard time sleeping. I kept asking God what I should do.

I've never had to reject someone on that level, especially as I am super loyal and fair. I also give many chances.

A week passed. A week and a half passed. At this point, I was livid.

I found out that she had an upcoming event at her shop where we could've begun promoting our items. What a great opportunity to introduce ourselves.

She didn't tell me anything.

How could she be my business partner? I knew her first business was her priority but I wasn't even asking for much!

I emailed her, texted her, etc., and still no reply...

Feeling helpless, I changed all the passwords that I could. What was left of my trust was now gone.

I felt like I made such a terrible judgment call. I honestly didn't know what she would do next and because I worked so hard, I didn't want what I created to be torn away from me.

Maternal Movement became part of my identity.

It took a while but we ended up having a heart to heart discussion and I ended up attending the event. I had hope that we had turned a corner and would no longer be in that dark valley. I believed Nelly understood. We were vulnerable and compassionate to each other.

I changed all the passwords back to what they were.

All went well for three days or so. It seemed like Nelly was back and was apologetic about ignoring me. She finally did something she promised to do for two or so months.

And then, dead silence again for almost five days.

I was heartbroken. My heart began to hurt again and I felt like I could no longer continue in this unhealthy relationship for me.

I couldn't control her in any way, and that drove me up the wall. I tried to hold it all in but it was bound to give at some point. My sense of fairness and principle just couldn't take this abuse any longer.

The day I finally broke it off with my partner, I had an early lunch with a friend and our kiddos.

I hate sharing my dirty laundry but I needed someone else's perspective.

I am very passionate and can react strongly, when I do react, so I needed to make sure I wasn't hasty.

My lovely friend Nikki, listened to my story patiently, after which she concurred that she, herself, would be going crazy, that this indeed was not a positive relationship and I had to do something about it.

I felt very shaken up. Confrontation is not in my nature. I tend to suffer in silence.

Some call me stoic. I call myself frozen. Emotions overwhelm me. I don't like falling to pieces.

Nikki gave me a beautiful leather bracelet with the word, Warrior, written on it.

After our lunch, I would keep looking at the bracelet, trying to gather the courage to be, indeed, that warrior.

My daughter and I went swimming at Fort Yargo that afternoon. It was a sunny day and the water was almost warm. Maya loved it. I couldn't get her out of the water! Purple lips or not, she was determined to be the little mermaid that day.

Sometime and somewhere between the sand, the sun and the lazy water, I gained a burst of courage. I knew that once and for all, I had to do something. I couldn't carry this leaden weight anymore. It was making me physically ill.

I had to give Nelly a way out. She may be saying that she's still in but I didn't see the commitment or the passion.

We were both on very different wavelengths.

So I sent her a text, to which she responded almost immediately! (I knew she could do it!)

Having not had a word back for almost five days, here she was, immediately upset, hurt and argumentative.

I don't blame her. No one likes being rejected.

But I didn't like it when she said I was ousting her at her weak point. It may have been true, but I was accommodating her weak points for months! I didn't blame her but I did believe that it wasn't the right time for her to be involved in something to which she clearly couldn't give much of herself.

She didn't refute that I've done the percentage I've mentioned before and that she was barely involved. Felt good to have that confirmation.

I finally told her that we all have problems, that's the common denominator on this planet.

And hey, I didn't ask much. I've carried her weight. I just needed to believe that my partner would be there, responsive. And Nelly wasn't. Especially, after our heart to heart... and nothing changed.

I've even invited her to come along to a UGA small business consulting meeting the following week, wanting to make sure she was satisfied and in case she needed to vent in front of a third party.

Nelly asked me why I'd offer that to her after ousting her. I replied that I so badly wanted to do the right thing, to be honorable, to give her every opportunity she needed or wanted.

We agreed that the next day I would pick up my items from her shop and I would pay her for the roll-ons and then our partnership would be over.

I felt saddened and liberated at the same time.

I went back to playing with my baby.

The next day, I've waited for her to show up at her shop around lunchtime.

As I've waited, I prayed I would be as kind and appropriate as possible in this very awkward situation.

I didn't mean to hurt her. We did have some good times but my passion and my drive had surpassed and surprised us both. I think we needed to have had chats to get to know one another rather than just jumping in together. I thought we had sufficient knowledge of each other but what happened between us proved to me that either I was bad at reading people or something seriously went wrong.

Her SUV rolled around the corner, parked, and she walked out with a very somber face. I hated seeing her so upset, but I've made the difficult decision, a decision I've later not regretted because I believe it was the right one for the type of company it was shaping up to be. And anyway, because of her lack of involvement it had the Olga flavoring all over it, and Nelly flavor would have had a very hard time breaking through. Not spicy enough.

We quickly and quietly exchanged the items. Maya grabbed a few items off the floor that were in the process of being packed away, which made Nelly tense in an already tension filled situation. I couldn't get Maya out of there quickly enough. In the midst of this, I tried to get my message across that when she is ready we could work together on a project or anything else that would serve us both, but as separate entities. I tried to make her feel better, but how realistic is it to expect to make someone feel better if you are the cause of their pain?

After this exchange, I met up with a friend at the Big City Bread Café. I really needed that time-out to chill out and center myself. As always, the rush hour was intense, and by intense I mean, the wait time in line took approximately half an hour, and then you had to wait for the food to come out as well. But nevertheless, the weather was sunny and I was starting to feel cheerful.

I learned my lesson. For me it was that I would never partner again. I am a type of person that is able to be the lone wolf. I can make my own decisions and stick to them. And although it may take longer alone, I will still get there with my sanity intact.

It took another week and a half for Nelly to let go of our Facebook group, which I've built up and was quite proud of. I was losing sleep, worrying that in anger she may delete the whole group altogether.

I've reminded her a few times to pass over the reins and nothing happened, until the very moment that I was sitting down, finally, in the wee hours of the day, to create a new group. I saw a text from the night before, stating simply, "done".

I honestly couldn't believe it was all over. Was I truly free to follow through on my vision and dream and goals that were shaping up before me? I could now take everything that grew out of my passion organically and shape it, fine-tune it, and make it impactful.

I thought I wouldn't see her for some time, running into her by happenstance in, maybe, half a year here and there, but boy was I wrong.

That same day, when I was finally and completely free to pursue my dreams unencumbered, I ran into her at the Bishop Park playground.

Maya ran out in front of me, otherwise I may have contemplated jumping back into the car and speeding away. It was still too new, too raw. I didn't know how Nelly would react.

I didn't want to upset her.

God, I prayed, what are you doing?

As I neared her, we greeted each other. I decided to speak honestly and told her how weird it felt to see her there, at that time, right after everything. I didn't want to be fake or pretend. I respected her enough to be completely honest.

Nelly was snippety at first, but then we both mellowed out as our kids continued to play together and hop around us. I like her kids, they are a fun bunch.

There was a moment when I thought we would separate and pretend to run after our kids, in the opposite directions, but our kids held us bound. I prayed again, and this time I decided to go with it. I trusted that God knew what He was doing.

The most incredible thing happened. In that space of honesty and being real, we ended up having a conversation that was so delightful, deep, healing, respectful, appreciative and engaging on many levels. I truly got to know her so much more, and I hope she understood me a bit more as well.

It got to the point where we both didn't want to leave, we were enjoying so much this long awaited-for connection. I was so happy and surprised to recognize that Nelly was indeed the great person that I took her for, from the very beginning.

Her ability to stay near me, talk with me and go past the very awkward situation to the real me, the core of who I was, proved to me that she indeed was special.

She has something that not many have. She has honor.

I am pleased that God knew best, and He knew this interaction would be good for the both of us, for us to see the person behind the partner role.

A month passed. At this point, I decided to send her a text, to see if perhaps she would like to hang out sometime, grab a coffee, etc. It didn't have to be soon. Maybe in a month or two? I wanted to give her more time to recover. She responded eagerly with a definitive yes, which made me very happy. A couple days later, I saw an invitation from Nelly to an event she was hosting.

If you are on the right path, God will even reconcile your enemies to you.

I don't know what went wrong, exactly. She's the right sort of person I would love to call my friend, but the wrong sort of business partner for me.

I am sure I am much to blame. I set my expectations too high, perhaps?

But, I've learned and I am ready to share.

Never give up hope

It's been a while, and now you've decided to dream again. Perhaps you are a mother like me, who thought that you would be completely satisfied within your established roles as a mother and a wife. You stay at home and you love the place where you live. Perhaps on the outside, everything is peachy and you should be super grateful for what you've got. And you've got plenty. You are frequently reminded of that, by the people that cannot understand what is going on in your heart.

The brazen thought, that perhaps this is not fulfilling enough, attempts to escape the lockbox where you stuffed it in, bolted by many strong locks.

I've been taught from a very early age what was expected of me, which often overlooked my intelligence, drive, passion, and interests.

My husband and I moved to Athens, GA, the day after we found out we were expecting. I just left a corporate job. Thoughts of a career and any other self-fulfilling tasks had evaporated with a vengeance.

When I gave birth, all I expected myself to want and be was a mother and a wife, for a while... perhaps a long while, but I couldn't escape this feeling that something inside of me was brewing like a volcano and needed to come out. It started to threaten my existence. It started to steal my peace.

I was embarrassed to admit that my life was not enough. That something else needed to fit into this equation. I struggled to make my husband understand that nothing is wrong with him or our life, that these sentiments were not his fault.

It took some time, but now I feel like he gets me, he is on my team.

When I was told to write out my list for the new year, it wasn't completely out of the blue.

Since August 2016, things were changing for my family. We felt a shift in the air. We started to believe again, to dream again, to reach for something higher.

When the year 2017 came around and things were rolling out so easily at first, I believed they would continue to be smooth, but they weren't.

You've read the big story but you don't know about the many little stories that happened along the way. The many disappointments and opportunities falling through. Ideas not working out in the way I hoped they would. How close I've come to selling out at times, hoping to get promoted by others, and at the last second learning to stay strong, and on point regarding my message, trusting that God would promote me, not people.

I still hoped.

When the team members that I gathered to be the content creators for the Maternal Movement got so fired up and then completely fizzled out, that hurt. But I had to trust God that He was the One filtering out the individuals that were meant to stay the course with me from the ones that didn't.

I've learned that everything truly does happen for a reason. The most enlightening lesson that I've learned along the way (you can read about the many more lessons in Living An Empowered Life Personally and Professionally) was that behind every setback is a setup.

Every... single... time...

You may not believe me now but once you start looking for the setups, you will start seeing them, and once you do, you will forever no longer be a victim of your circumstance.

Plans will fall through. People will fail you. Some people won't care about your message, but you must always be strong. You must always believe that you have something of incredible value. No one else can do it the way you can.

Be dedicated to your dream. Love it, nurture it, devote yourself to it.

Since I began to dream again and follow through on my desires, around February of 2017, I worked at growing Maternal Movement, and increasing my sphere of influence every single day. Yes, every single day, I do something, small or big, to get me a step closer to the culmination of my goals. Every single day. You may be intimidated by that statement but don't be. Once you find out what you love so much with such passion and intention, you will want to work on it… every single day.

I had to take intentional time-outs because I was wearing myself out without noticing.

If you are a Christian, you've got nothing to lose. You've already gained everything you need in Jesus Christ. So why try so hard? Because you don't want to bury what He has given you, talents and gifts that would make this world a much better place. He wants to work through you, in you, and through others around you. You must give Him the space to do what must be done.

Everything I do is all about showing my dedication to Him. I believe He has a vision of greatness set before me, an ordinary mama, of ordinary means and a super ordinary, poor mentality upbringing.

In my weakness, He shows His strength. And believe me, He has plenty of opportunities to show His strength!

I've also seen a pattern in life. The greater the opposition that you experience in life, the greater the call on your life may be. You may have such a powerful and divine purpose set out before you that the atmosphere of this time may be suppressing you, stifling you. But don't you quit! Lean into God.

Never, ever give up hope. You will get there. You will make it.

And you will not fail. Success is your only destiny if you are consistent and persistent, and forever hopeful!

You may have to make a million mistakes, I've made plenty. I went into a sphere of influence I knew nothing about. I had to set up a website, Facebook pages, ads, groups, stores, learn Instagram, YouTube and Twitter, and get over being shy on videos. Most of the time I was learning as I was doing it, whatever it was.

I just went for it. I didn't want to lose my momentum, constantly being propelled by my passion and my desire to share with other moms that they've got something very special inside them. That the world needs them. That I find them incredibly valuable and they need to treat themselves right!

I am an all or nothing kind of person. And in the midst of my journey, I find myself giving all I've got. The trick is on us. The more we give, the more it grows! I've learned that there is no end to the capacity within us when we are on the right path, when we are inspired.

I had to learn to define and redefine my message and what I was selling. We are all selling something to an extent. I learned that I want to inspire, empower and engage the mamas within their communities and spheres of influence.

I want to help other women to find their dreams and spread their message. I want my content creators to have greater exposure and demand for what they are so passionate about.

I want a community of women to rise up and inspire the whole world!

I love the mama dreamer. I love the mama doer. But can we have a mama that can do both? Sure we can.

It just takes a bit of focus. A lot of grit. A few tears, many sighs and a couple of "well done's".

Many say, find a job you love and you will never work a day in your life.

That's not true. You WILL work, maybe harder than ever before, but you will LOVE it, and that's what makes it so worth it.

If we love something, it gives us strength, drive, perseverance and motivation.

Find your Why and you will find the What, When, Where and How.

I am so blessed that although I am leading Maternal Movement alone, I am not truly alone. I've met incredible women from all over the USA. They inspire me when I feel low. They infuse me with their enthusiasm, their persistence in achieving the goals they've set before them.

Because of Maternal Movement, I've had opportunities come up where I am now able to spread my message on a bigger scale. My writing had touched people when I even had no idea that it did. I've had people tell me that I've inspired them in one way or another. I've been asked to speak, to write for others and to create videos.

I love the women of this generation. They are hungry and thirsty, and there is nothing wrong with that.

We are hungry to leave a legacy for our children and thirsty to make a difference in this much depreciated world.

If that is wrong, I'd rather be wrong than right.

I see no other choice for us. We must stand up for a better tomorrow because, as every woman that brought a child into this world, knows... we still have hope.

Get your priorities straight and take that first step

I've written on this topic in my first book, this book being my second, but I find that I must share this principle with you. I want you to know that you will be making sacrifices but gaining so much more in the end.

Once you find your Why, everything else will fall into place: the what, when, where, and how.

For me, my Why is my daughter. The What is the legacy I want to leave behind for her.

I've told my husband that I cannot teach my daughter through words only, she needs me to be an example. How can I tell her to speak her mind and to share her valuable self with the world, when I've done neither? How can I tell her to follow her dreams when I didn't? Would she find me believable? So my legacy to her is a woman that she can imitate, all the lessons I've learned and the lifestyle I am imparting to her, all of my achievements, my ceiling becoming her floor.

The When for me became, right now. What can I do now? And then it just goes on from there, until the day I die, I want to be creating a legacy, a strong and powerful influence, of which she can be proud of and will be able to transfer onwards to her own children.

The Where became the place where I am, my home. Because of the internet, all I need is a laptop, a cell phone and a car for a few meetings here and there. In all fairness, for me, the Where became everywhere. I am always working wherever I am, either physically or in my head.

My husband tells me to turn my brain off, but I just cannot!

By nature, I am a thinker, so I cannot always wind-down easily. Had to learn what works for me in that department.

The How was a bit harder for me to figure out. How do I deliver my message? I made a few mistakes but also learned a few tricks along the way.

Because initially I thought we had a physical shop, Maternal Movement was beginning to focus on creating merchandise to spread the message but after that space was gone, those efforts were derailed.

I decided to write my first book. The message was solid but the people weren't buying it. I was an unknown entity.

I had to learn what works for me on social media, and even though I felt I was doing everything right, the results were not where I wanted them to be. I thought that surely everyone could relate to having a dream, a passion, a desire for fulfillment, but very few actually do. It saddens me to say this but many people have trampled on their dreams for so long, ignored the call of the heart, that inside of them everything is dry and dead.

It doesn't have to be. You can reignite your fires. The first step is to be willing.

Once you have your mechanisms figured out, you will need to focus on what will help you get where you need to go. Don't invest yourself in time consuming efforts that will not get you there, only if they are very fun and you are in a dire lack of fun time.

Don't overschedule yourself with other mamas and activities you were guilt-tripped into participating.

Create a specific time you will focus on achieving your goals every single day, or five out of seven. Stick to that plan no matter what. Make appointments in the afternoon if you work in the mornings.

Find quotes or inspirational content regularly, anything that will keep your fire flaming.

I also find it very useful to have an accountability group with whom you can share your challenges and your successes, a group of people that will cheer you on and give you a kick when you need it.

I've recently started a secret mastermind group on Facebook, through which I can connect with an amazing bunch of ladies, whom I am proud to call friends.

Trust me, when you work on your goals, day in and day out, eventually it becomes a habit and a desire, if it wasn't so at first. Miss a day, or God forbid, two, and you will find yourself all over the place, restless to get back to that place of creativity and follow-through.

If you want to live like no one else, you will have to do things that no one else does. If you want to be great, you cannot do ordinary things.

I keep thinking of how amazing it will be to give back to the causes I care about so deeply. About ways I can change things and get involved. You cannot do that if you don't have influence, money or both.

Sometimes you may have more than one Why and that is great, because if one Why doesn't seem to be as important one day, the other Why's will carry you through.

What do you do next? It all starts with a small step.

It may be a shaky step, a step without fear or trepidation, an ordinary step, a step of joy, a step of indecision, but a step nevertheless.

A baby takes the first step and no matter how weak or strong that step is, the joy of empowerment is quite obvious! They did it! If they can do this one step, where will two or three take them? What if we chain the steps together, what will happen then?

And off they go! And this is where the story takes another turn. The baby now can explore and enjoy the new freedom and learn what it means to have a place in the world on another level. Soon enough, they will run and bike and drive a car, maybe fly a plane.

We all start off as babies, in life and in everything we do. And that's absolutely normal, to be expected and not to be embarrassed about. Every successful person, believe it or not, had to start off as a baby in their field and then they took steps... And the steps took them everywhere!

There is nothing special about them in comparison to you. The only difference may be is that they took that first step and then continued to add on. Consistency is key.

Persistence in spite of opposing forces is the lifeblood of success.

Look, if they can do it, so can you.

Nothing is impossible.

Any promotion, any endeavor can be obtained and achieved, step at a time.

Before we go any further, I want you to internalize this truth: success at the expense of health and family is not real success. As long as you have these parameters in line, you've got balance. Keep this truth in mind, often, and make sure that this part of the equation is always satisfied. If they fall short, you will never enjoy your success the way you hoped you would.

If you have your health (physical, emotional, spiritual) and your family balanced, you are already wealthy and your steps may be less fickle, less wobbly because you have the self-confidence and the support of your family.

I strongly believe that if you take the right steps, consistent and persistent steps, you will get there.

Our dreams are there for a reason. Our talents are ours for a reason as well. Why?

Because they are meant to be ours, to be enjoyed, employed, and achieved.

It is very simple. Once we take the simplicity out of success, forget it. That's when it gets complicated.

So let's go back to the small step that I take every single day that sets me up for grander steps. I make my coffee. I bring it upstairs. Set it down. Fuss around with my kiddo. Then I take my first sip. That's the trigger point for me. I am settling down to business (as much as I possibly can, in spite of controlled chaos around me).

My first step each day is my sip of coffee. Then I get out my laptop or phone, whichever is easier to use at that moment.

I know that once I take out my "power" tools, I better be getting my head in the game. And even if I don't feel like it, I still do it. Because I believe that every step I take in the direction of my dreams, it counts.

What makes a person successful? Their ability to believe that every step they take will bring them closer to the culmination point, despite opposition, in spite of others' disbelief, regardless of the lack of reward.

There is a quote that I read in school, many years ago, that will stay with me for life.

"Failure is 100% guaranteed if you do nothing." Then do something! Each step you take will increase your chances of success. I think it is worth trying, at least!

But try it for a month. Make a game out of it. Each day, take small steps, or if you can, big steps when you feel comfortable. Visualize yourself moving closer and closer. Feel the destination. See it, taste it, enjoy it. It can surely be yours.

Nothing is out of your reach. Nothing is too high up, or too far out. If that was the case, we wouldn't be flying today, or enjoying our sweet little laptops.

If it is out there, it can be yours. If it is just an idea, it can materialize. All that we see around us was once an idea and now, an idea manifested.

Go for that small step. Then take a next one.

You never know, you might just... like it.

Who do you want to be?

Some of us can easily say who we want to be like, some cannot, some don't care and some, like me, will say that they want to be a better version of themselves.

In that case, what's your version like? Imagine that version, make it a part of yourself, study it and dream on it.

The next step would be to act, dress, talk, think and move forward as that version of you would, like the person that you imagine you would be, at the end of your journey, and at your destination.

For me, what often works and gives me an added boost of confidence, is to envision myself as that version that had achieved all of her dreams and goals, a version that is extremely brave, kind and generous.

Because Maternal Movement started out as a fitness class idea, for which I did indeed create a specific formula, like no other class you've ever encountered, I began to imagine myself as a fitness instructor.

When the space to hold the class evaporated, along with my partner's shop, I had to scramble quickly to redefine the company and myself.

Having said that, I do want to bring up an example when imagining myself as a fit and confident instructor led me to go out and buy a few colorful sporty outfits. As I began to wear them, I began to feel like that version of myself. I began to want to workout a bit more intensely. Because I was feeling more fit, I began to imagine myself as a more fit and slim person.

A slim person would eat less, for starters. So I easily transitioned into eating a little less here and there. Those small changes led me to make a few more smaller changes, and voila!, I lost weight and became more fit!

And it all started with just visualizing a version of myself that emphasized a particular characteristic.

Visualizing myself in a specific way led me to an increase of many other powerful characteristics such as bravery, generosity, forgiveness, perseverance, to name a few.

And no, this doesn't mean that I am faking it. It means I am wisely investing into my future and recognizing that I am a work in progress and that shaping and molding of myself is within my rights and ability.

I approach everything as if I am already mega successful. Who wouldn't want to do business with me? Who wouldn't want to spend time with me? I feel quite valuable.

 When I visualize myself as the person that had already achieved her dreams, I can more quickly forgive others and not take what they do against me so personally. I don't have to compete with them, but only with myself.
What happens if something falls through? A person renegaded on their commitment to me? A deal that went nowhere? Because I already see myself as if I had achieved my objectives, I am not hung up on it. I shrug off these occurrences and can be quite understanding and merciful because I am not dependent on them for my success.

It is truly liberating.

Being liberated from holding onto no-go situations allows me to be authentic with everyone.

I don't need to convince them to follow me. I would love it if they went along with me on this amazing journey, but not at the expense of losing myself in the incessant harrowing of unrelenting tactics.

Because I don't let myself wallow in the negative, I consistently have the drive to try again. I am full of energy because my mission fuels my vision. I constantly see in my mind's eye what I believe is coming my way.

Because I imagine myself to already be that person, the one that achieved her dreams, I act like that person. I walk with confidence. I walk with joy and pride. I feel more compassionate and accommodating, generous and supportive of other people's journeys.

The most fun part about this lesson? People treat you the way you treat yourself. People see you the way you see yourself.

In the very least, fake it 'till you make it.

When I felt sad, I would oftentimes go to the mirror and smile at myself. That tricks the brain to believe that I am fine. And if that didn't work, most often I would find myself laughing at my silly self, and that for sure would perk up my spirits.

I can tell that if you have read thus far, you are a very driven and motivated person.

That's half the battle won already.

Don't let the other half be lost by quitting or losing passion.

See yourself as a winner.

A winner doesn't quit. A winner, wins... eventually.

Take the time to invest in your dreams, adjust your thinking, visualize yourself accomplishing everything you are setting out to do.

At the end of the day, no one is truly in your way, except for you.

Win the battle in your head and you will win the battle for success, without a doubt.

In the next section I will share with you a few more lessons and tips that helped me discover MY formula for a passionate life!

Slow down

Are you surprised yet? Slow down?! Did you feel like you were set up to gear up and gallop away? I'm sure you weren't expecting me to say, slow down, at this time in the book.

My dear lady, only when you have learned the value of slowing down and the ability to do it, can you successfully grasp the concept of hitting it hard!

If you keep moving at a fast pace, knocking out appointments left and right, you may be missing out on the joy that happens in those everyday moments.

A few days ago, I learned the value of slowing down, because it hit me deeply, this realization that I was indeed going very fast.

Things weren't going completely right that morning. Nor did they go that well after this particular event but I did have something to work with for a few days.

I was getting Maya ready quickly, in order to meet someone at the park, a potential collaborator on a project for my newly developing business, after which I had to rush her to gymnastics.

I was already running late because of Maya's inability to eat on time and because of our issue with the status of our washer's delivery.

So there I am, changing her diaper, which is never easy because she just cannot be bothered to lay still, and fitting clothes onto her moving body, when my dear hubby decides to have a leisurely chat with me.

I let out staccato phrases. Short remarks. Clean cut words.

What he asked me next blew me away.

"Why are you so angry?"

To which I responded in shock, " I'm not angry, I'm just busy!"

So yes, this exchange was later hashed out with a few more mamas, who, by the way, all ended my aforementioned sentence, as in, fill-in-the-blank, I'm just... busy!

So there, men may never understand, but we sure can make them try. One wise lady told me to tell him to treat my time at home as my office space. I wouldn't take up his time chit-chatting while visiting his office at a time when he is busy, would I?

And how about another phrase, "You aren't in a rush, are you?" Um, most of the time, I am.

I do have a set schedule each day, without which I don't feel productive. So yes, I do have tasks and goals, which give me a semblance of meaning and accomplishment. And yes, so many tasks fall on us, women, because a woman at home must somehow earn her keep. She must raise her children well: take care to make sure their little brains develop optimally, they get plenty of social time and sunshine, be entertained with various educational activities, eat well, sleep well, look clean, which is impossible!, and at the same time, take care of the home, the gardens, pet, husband, and make homemade meals.

Good grief, she must also look presentable and happy. She tries to take care of herself and exercises when she gets the chance. She tries to make some time to relax, but again, most of the downtime is spent either with her husband ... or, what was I thinking, 99% of it is spent with the husband, so she barely has any downtime.

If she is like me, a woman that fills up her glass when she has time to ponder the mysteries of life on her own, in quiet solitude, good luck!

Don't get me started if that woman also wants to pursue her passions and dreams!

When do you do that? At 3:00 a.m. in the morning, like me?

By the way, that type of lifestyle is not the healthiest. Trust me.

The next day is just a waste of lethargy, exhaustion and numbness to any new opportunities.

It's all in the moments

Now that I've frightened you, silly, I will retrace my steps and start off again with that simple concept: slow down.

I feel your panic. How will you fit anything into your day if you indeed slow down?

There's the magic, slowing down while cultivating a sense of appreciation, passion and joy, makes the time stand still, even in that brief moment. Get enough moments like this into your day and you will feel fulfilled as if you took a vacation.

For example, feel your child's hair when you hold her tight. Hold that hug a little longer and breathe in the child's sweet scent. Hold his hand a little tighter and feel, truly feel, the texture of the hand. Take five minutes to cuddle. Or to look out the window, watching the birds, a warm beverage in hand. Go outside in the morning, smell the freshness of the new day. Read your favorite book for a few minutes, listen to your favorite song.

Learn what small moments make your day feel so big, so complete. Fill your day with little moments that bring you joy.

Wear that pretty blouse. You've got one life to live, might as well enjoy it.

Put on that bright lipstick.

You are worth it. Make the time for yourself. When there's a will, there's a way. That's not a wasted phrase. That's true.

Having moments that fill up your cup is not a pretty accessory, it is a necessity. I find that the more tense I am, the more stressed I am, that I am more apt to be what I never wanted to be: a wound-up-tight mama that shouts at her kid. So, no, time-outs are not only for children. They are a teaching tool for the adults as well.

One of my favorite time-outs was the beach. No other place on Earth was able to do as great of a job de-stressing me and refreshing my spirit. Unfortunately, it no longer is. Maya is constantly on the move. After three hours of constant activity, I am so exhausted and in need of a nap!

Hey, this phase of life will not last forever, so I might as well love it the way it is, and find alternatives that will suffice for now.

Currently, instead of the beach, the most relaxing and refreshing activity I can do is go outside and sit on our swinging bench, drink next to me and book in hand, relax in the sun and the Georgia heat. That will have to do for now. The silver lining here is that I can go outside every day versus going to the beach, which is no longer restorative for me.

Do what works for you. Also, remember, whatever you do, if it isn't a problem for you, it isn't a problem, even if others say it otherwise.

For my peace of mind, presently, I have to allow Maya to take a nap in my bed, with me in it... and remain there until she falls asleep. I cannot let her cry it out, because she will never stop. She is that determined to get her way.

So napping in the crib will wait. Perhaps she will return on her own. At first it was a problem for me, but soon enough, I redefined what was happening and eliminated this problem through the power of perception.

Eliminate the stressors, pick your battles wisely, and just let go. Life will never be perfect. We surely aren't, and that's ok.

Set your priorities straight

Sometimes when we are rushing, we fail to see the opportunities around us or to glean a bit of wisdom through observation. Being busy is so celebrated and I fell for it. It created a sense of structure for me, I knew what I was doing each moment.

The funny part was, I was doing so much and yet had very little to show for my time.

I had to take a time-out from life to re-evaluate my priorities.

I knew I had to learn to be disciplined, yet, flexible. I needed to schedule-in time to just be, to just see what happens in that hour, to let myself do whatever I wanted (provided I could do that with a kid in tow). And yes, sometimes I had to let my child watch a bit of TV so I could get a breather, and be a better mom for it.

I've learned the value of getting unhurried. I strive to have the right balance each week.

Sometimes I have to clean less because I'd rather spend that time on my child or my hot and leisurely bath, because my sanity is worth every bit of that sweat.

I've learned to prioritize better according to my values and the needs of that week. At times, I had to say no to social outings and sacrifice a few walks with the girls because I knew I could use that time to further my dreams.

If you were a brand, what is it that you would be selling? Because that is what we are selling our children.

What is your message? Focus on the activities that will support your message in life.

Prioritize what is non-negotiable for you. The negotiable can follow suit after your non-negotiable items. You only have so much time in the day. Focus on what truly matters.

Have some fun, woman - thrive!

If you find yourself not enjoying life at this moment, dull and exhausted, do this...

If you can, drop everything immediately and do something fun, this instant! Having fun is not just for children. It restarts us and gives us not only a brighter perspective but also a new reserve of energy.

Nelly and I were bogged down with paperwork one day. During our meeting, I whipped out oils that I brought from home and said, "Hey, let's do something fun! Let's create a Motivated Mama natural perfume with a few essential oils." And so, we did. We had so much fun going down this unplanned and unexpected route that it not only re-enthused us to move further but also brought out a few more fresh ideas.

Sometimes in slowing down, in the stillness, or while having fun, our very best ideas can pop up freely. A passionate woman, a wise woman, will learn how to make each moment of life a little more fun, a bit more enjoyable, a bit more palatable.

If it's fun and brings you joy, do it.

Remember, the more fun you have doing things, the more joy you tend to get out of whatever you are doing!

Cultivate a lifestyle of fun! Take a time-out to have fun in the midst of something that is super tedious and boring. We all have to deal with the realities of life!

If you are a lover of dancing and music, whip those out as frequently as you can. Dance a little... or a lot. Be silly. Shout out the words! Music is a balm to the soul. Find music that you enjoy. Don't be afraid to sing off tune. Live a little.

Now, let's talk about thriving!

I now know what it means to thrive, instead of strive - the secret of happiness!

I will spare you the details but there were a few instances that dropped me very low, in the midst of feeling a great high on life. I was so upset that these moments were able to catapult me into depths of despair. I vowed to discover the power over this phenomenon. I didn't want to be at the mercy of circumstance and people.

A few hours of being deep in thought led me to the conclusion that I based a lot of my happiness on the specific outcomes, actions of people and the way people thought of me.

These inputs into my life I clearly couldn't control, so if I gave away my power to these variables, by golly, my life would constantly be a roller coaster of ups and downs.

If you base your success on others' opinions, forget it. You will not rest. You will be up so high and low so quickly that not only will your head spin, but your heart will not have the time to settle down either.

For me, as a Christian, dis-attaching from uncontrollable outcomes was easy. I now base my happiness on something always constant and always there for me, God, who never changes. I can always count on Him. He always gets my passions and fuels my dreams. I no longer worry about what others think of me, because what truly matters is what He thinks of me.

And I know what He thinks of me. He loves me so much that He sacrificed His own son to bring me life with an abundance. He wants to give me hope and a blessed future.

<u>Go outside</u>

Sweet mama, I may not be an expert on many things, but I will tell you this, nature has a way of healing many wounds and restoring many a tired heart.

At this moment, I am writing outside in my backyard. I hear the lovely melody of birds chirping away, sunshine all around me and my child making a crazy racket here and there, toys aflutter and shouts carried on the breeze.

It's peaceful even though I've been interrupted multiple times since I've started writing this section.

Yes, I've had to redefine moments according to my new standard of living, one that includes my daughter. It isn't always easy, in fact, it rarely is, but with every perceived accomplishment, my ability to function amidst distractions and noise has been reaching higher and higher levels.

It is no longer an excuse to say, hey, I've got a child or children, I cannot slow down, EVER! Not true. You can and you will. You are going to realize the value of slowing down because, in the long run, that is what will give you the energy to speed up.

I keep looking around my backyard, various sections are homes to bushes of roses, grasses, shrubs, trees and various flowers. I am so proud of what I have achieved here.

For many years, I've been saddled with the worst case of everything opposite of a green thumb. It is only now, and because of letting go of false beliefs and acquiring the belief that I am great at growing life, my plants are thriving and giving me the joy and pleasure I've seen others privy to.

Did you know that the frequency that trees and plants give out can be mimicked by our body when we are surrounded by them? That is the reason you feel so good walking through the woods. So calm. So relaxed. Your body aligns with the tune of nature. The color green boosts our creative powers as well.

Not only green is the symbolic color of life, it will also give life to new ideas, inspirations and dreams.

I strongly recommend spending some time outdoors each day. If you can, plant a garden, dig around in the dirt, feel rooted to the Earth. Connect with Life.

Each time that I pluck out the weeds from the flower beds, I am reminded to pluck out the ideas or thoughts that are taking root, but aren't there to serve me, but to override the beauty of the flowers, bushes, shrubs, and grasses that were meant to thrive, unencumbered, with access to perfect freedom.

Learn from nature. Our minds and our lives are beautiful plant beds that need constant attention, weeding, water, food, sunshine.

We all need sunshine, physical and emotional. We need the love of the people we are surrounded by. Especially by our own very selves. Show love to the real you.

Feed yourself thoughts and actions that are nourishing for you, life giving.

If you start allowing the weeds to grow, they will dominate your joy systems. Pluck them out while they are young. Don't allow thoughts of failure, self-flagellation, and lack to grow.

If you can, take the nature inside with you as well. Fill your home with pots brimming with leafage or cacti, whatever is your fancy, or whatever it is that can actually survive in your household.

Nurture the life outside and inside yourself. Nurture the life outside and inside your home.

Create an oasis in your home

It is no accident that your home is either a mess or a neat freak show. It may depend, to an extent, on what your time allowance is and how crazy wild your kids are, but... and this is true and I cannot make excuses for myself anymore, I've noticed a huge correlation between what is going on in my head and how my house tends to look inside.

When things are going well, my priorities are taken care of and I feel fulfilled on my path, my home looks much more inviting, calming and inspiring.

As soon as something gets out of balance, I can tell immediately. My home shows it. There are messes like piled up laundry, dishes in the sink and disorganized items all over the place.

Having noticed this pattern, I've started to empower my brain, using a similar trick to smiling in the mirror at yourself even though you are sad, to achieve the result I need.

If I need inspiration and productivity to occur, I clean my home. I clean at least something, or a particular area that needs a pick me up. Accomplishing a simple goal like that, seeing the before and after, helps me to realize that I can do the same in other areas of my life. There is a tremendous sense of accomplishment when you live in an environment you actually enjoy.

According to Tatyana Pyshnyak, from Voice Interiors, "It's hard to downsize, simplify, or eliminate when our mindsets have been set on acquiring, purchasing, and just plain more, more, and more. The media, culture, and modern way of life unfortunately can lead to the clutter in our homes. Try simplifying and paring it down to basics, which will allow you to focus on quality time with your family, rather than cleaning, managing, and organizing the various messes."

What you have around you will permeate the structure of who you are. It is not a lie, and science proves that colors and shapes, scents and textures can affect how we feel.

If you are at a loss at how to go about creating a particular feel for your home, find a talented interior decorator/designer to whom you can entrust this task or work closely with.

"Less and less we rely upon our own skills and talents to design fashion, build furniture, plant flowers, and paint paintings. Someone else is doing it for us. All we need can be bought with a simple click of the mouse. Perhaps we are stuck in the world of consumerism and take the easy way out. We consume, but do not create. Maybe we need to embrace simplicity and get engaged with our surroundings. Maybe we just need to get inspired (T.P., Voice Interiors)."

Your home is your domain. You are in charge and you are ultimately responsible for how you feel in that environment. Don't take your home for granted. You spend so much time there, it is worth it to put an extra effort in creating something your whole family can appreciate and enjoy.

Listen to your body

I've known this before but I've really internalized this concept only in the last few days. My body talks.

It really does.

A couple of weeks ago, I've set out to do my usual HIIT exercises, which work tremendously, by the way. As I was about to whip them out, my body rebelled.

Something that I tend to enjoy so much became so very violently unpleasant to me.

All out of the blue, my body simply screamed, STOP!

I stood there, knowing I couldn't start.

It was a sudden surprise to me.

After a few minutes, I decided to go along with this temperamental state and asked myself, what would I prefer to do instead? I could hear my inner self telling me that what I truly needed at that moment was a session on the elliptical with my most favorite music.

I haven't been on the elliptical for many months.

That week, most of my sessions ended up being on the elliptical, my music full blast.

The next week, I started to get the sense that my body was trying to tell me something else. So I quieted myself and listened.

It quietly told me that it would be very happy with a few yoga sessions.

So I did just that.

And then I started mixing them up.

And here I am. I still no longer have any desire to go back to HIIT, but I have a sense that soon I will be adding something else to my repertoire.

What have I learned? That my body needs a break and variety? Yes, that's true.

But there's a much bigger picture here that is hiding behind the veil.

There's a much deeper mystery within this quite typical story.

I decided to examine my weeks and noticed a very precise correlation between my mental state and the preferred method of exercise.

So, what happened? What happened was this, the day when unexpectedly I could no longer bring myself to perform my favorite exercises, my mind and emotions were so exhausted and so spent that I had no energy left that I could pour out from within. I could no longer go all out, nor focus on the steps to be taken. I had a lack within my spirit, soul and body.

Why was I attracted to the elliptical? Because in doing a repetitive task, I didn't have to think. I could just be. Why did I want my favorite music? Simply because it made me happy.

My lack needed to be filled, in this case, exhaustion of mind and emotion needed to be taken care of. My mind could relax and my emotions could become stimulated to ring out a higher frequency which would bring me out of the doldrums.

After a week or so of this treatment, I was finally able to do yoga.

I couldn't do it before because I was so unprepared to be left with my thoughts, I didn't want to face them.

During the turbulent, emotional time, the elliptical served its purpose, held me through it, as I rebuilt myself.

As I became stronger, and mentally fit, I began to crave yoga. I was no longer scared of my thoughts. I craved the slowing down and settling into a challenging pose.

I was able to work through my emotions.

Our bodies are so incredible!

They are a wonderful portrayal of what is happening on the inside. They channel the inner being.

I've written before how I've lost weight simply because I started seeing myself differently and going after my dreams. An inner weight was lifted, which resulted in a clear, physical manifestation.

Listen to your body. Go with it, not against it. It has a wisdom of the ages, an imprint of God.

I am so glad that I did what I did.

My physical expression and the proper response to my body's needs accelerated the healing of my inner self.

If I rebelled, I don't think I would be in this space of contentment.

Your body is your friend. It is not the enemy. It loves you. It wants to help you heal, to experience life on an optimum level.

Learn to get along. Treat yourself kindly.

Love your body. And if you cannot do that just yet, learn to respect what it has done for you already.

And finally, have a little trust

I've listed a few methods that will help you slow down and become in tune with what you need at this moment to recharge and to be ready for the next phase of speeding up!

Create a list that would be personal to you. Do as many life-boosting activities as you can. Learn to use all of your senses. You cannot do that if you rush around. Go for the feel, taste, scent, sight, and touch. The more you develop those senses, the more in tune you will be with your self, but most importantly you will be in touch with your environment, inner or outer.

When you know how to affect your inner or outer environments, how to adjust the course of your being, how to affect your mood and your drive, you will be capable to handle inputs and outputs of your being when things are coming at you at warp speed.

It is very important to realize that in slowing down we receive the energy to speed up.

If we are constantly speeding up, our reserves will become depleted eventually, our momentum will suffer and the breakdown of our selves will be inevitable.

Have a bit of trust in your self. Listen to your wisdom. Listen to that still small voice. You already know what it is that you must do at this time and how to spend that time most wisely and effectively. No one is able to give you the answers you precisely need all the time. We can share what worked for us, but it is up to you to figure out what works for you.

And I know you will. I pray that you will gain the knowledge you need to steer yourself in the proper direction at all times.

Speed up!

I've often shared that one must be always open to new opportunities or ways of doing something better. There is nothing vain or selfish to that concept. It can only improve your life and the lives of the ones you love most.

As soon as you start pursuing your dreams with a passion, you will encounter opposition, pain, fatigue, hurt, discouragement and so much more.

It will take everything you have at times to move one foot in front of the other, to believe that it can and WILL happen for you.

I've learned a few lessons that will help you quickly get out of the negative emotional zone and into a positive productive space where you don't have to relinquish your joy, your peace and your life.

With a few of these tricks up your sleeve, you will only get stronger, happier, and more accomplished!

Behind Every Setback is a Setup

Things won't always go your way but you must have faith that behind every setback there is a setup.

I've had an epiphany overcome me, so strongly and so completely.

I didn't see it as a tide coming in over on the horizon. Nor did I hear the roar of thunder letting me know that lightning was coming.

It was such a sudden occurrence, with an impact of a tsunami or a brazen earthquake. It destroyed my previously well-established thoughts on life.

I used to believe that I had to be brave each time I encountered a setback, to be patient, that things would turn around.

I knew that out of the bad, good things may happen as well, but I missed a crucial point, a law of the universe.

Behind every setback is a setup.

Looking back upon my life, I can see where I subconsciously took advantage of the bad times to catapult the energy of the moment into something more productive, more effective, and more palatable for me.

Imagine what I would have been able to achieve if I consciously was aware and was seeking out that setup?
Sure, you may be doubting me at this moment, but look at it this way... If you believe that pills can induce a placebo effect, how much more so would hope!

Even if my point isn't true, your belief in the truth of my statement would make it true in your life.

Perhaps next time I should write about the effect of faith on the human psyche!

Let me share with you how I came to possess this valuable knowledge.

It all started with a series of events that occurred to me over a period of about a month.

Things just weren't going my way.

I was so upset with a particular person, that they weren't behaving the way I wanted them to. Ergo, Ego moment.

No matter how I urged them, no matter what I did, I couldn't control the outcomes of that person.

I was super frustrated.

So, I started channeling that energy into something productive, something that made me happy and at the same time was a wonderful creative outlay.

Because of my frustration and pent up energy, my first book was created. Every note that was written, was birthed with passion from every moment that taught me something, or inspired me to be the person I wanted to be, someone free, to whom success is accessible no matter what stands in her way.

I was very proud of my book, but things weren't falling into place the way I could see them in my mind's eye, so I started looking for ways to control inputs into my life and my outputs, so that I could be at peace, filled with joy and freedom to thrive, not strive.

This is the pivotal moment in my story.

It hit me hard when I realized that my setback was actually a setup that gave life to my first book.

Because of this awareness, I started to look for that setup behind my current setback.

Soon, increasingly, ideas and connections started to appear to me and it became clear that the more I began to search for the setups, the more frequently I began to encounter them.End result? Out of a tempestuous situation, one that drove me crazy because I just couldn't control it, because of which, if I remained in that state of mind, I felt my success would be minimized greatly; I was squeezed out into a field of freedom.

I was able to transfer my energy from one platform to another, which suits my temperament and dreams a whole lot better.

Now I am looking forward to every challenge in my way because with my transformational thinking, I know I will end up being better off no matter what happens.

I am not afraid of my future. I am not anxious about what comes next because my mind is so trained to start looking around a problem, or a huge boulder in my way.

It will even find a way to walk through it, no doubt.

If you are a Christian, you already know that for the ones that love Him, everything will be made to work out for our good.

I knew this, but unfortunately, I never truly accepted that truth into my heart, my spirit.

If it weren't for my very emotional time, a struggle of the soul, I wouldn't be where I am today.

I wouldn't trade that experience for anything.I've learned a lesson that is more valuable than gold.

A lesson that will not only change my life, but yours as well!

Live well and prosper!

With every NO you will only get stronger

I wanted to do a reading at the Avid bookstore, in Athens, GA. Meticulously, I filled out the online forms for that event. I was super proud of the lessons I've learned and written about in my book, Living an Empowered Life Personally and Professionally: a collection of notes that will change your life. A couple of days passed and I received a kind email saying that although the book seemed great but, unfortunately, they will have no audience for it. So they wished me a very happy life and sent me on my way.

I could have been very upset, but I wasn't. Why? Because I was trained at this point to look for a setup. I started looking around in that situation and I realized that I will never be a victim again.

So I said to myself, from now on, with every NO I will only get stronger. That thought came to me fifteen minutes into my Zumba workout DVD.

I love exercise. Many epiphanies come to me while I am exercising. Movement is a beautiful thing!

So going back to that epiphany, I thought, what can I do at this moment that would empower me? What would be a strong move?

After my exercise of fifty-five minutes, super proud of that, by the way!, I ran upstairs to email Avid back with a different proposal. They may say yes, or maybe, no, but what matters to me is that I've tried, gave it my all, and didn't crumble at the signs of opposition.

Again, having the hope that things will eventually work out for my good, gives me the strength to move forward with determination rather than fall prey to weakness and despondence.

You will hear many No's on your way to getting "there", a mysterious state that we hope will fulfill our sense of accomplishment and self-realization.

I sure did. There were times I didn't know what to do with my inventory because it just didn't sell. Apparently, when you start out, you aren't a well-known entity, so no one gives a peach about your products or message.

Cultivating a following is one of the hardest achievements. Looking at the members leaving my group is not at the top of my list of fun things to witness. But I had to learn to never quit because quitters never win and winners never quit.

I've learned to respect the ones that made it, or on the way there, so much more. Everyday they have to wake up, pull themselves together and work towards their dream.

They have to be strong enough to handle criticism when they are at their most vulnerable state. Sharing yourself with the world opens you up to so much hurt, but only if you let them.

Learn to value yourself and be proud for taking every step, and I mean every step! Two steps forward and one step back. Three steps forward and two steps back. You cannot fail if you are learning in every step of the way.

Train your brain to embrace every setback, every NO, with a loud, YES!

Yes, to being stronger, wiser and braver.

Let me tell you something. The biggest No's you will ever encounter are the No's within your own head. Those are the No's, once overcome, that will result in you becoming stronger than ever, unshakeable, quite capable, and immensely successful.

Halfway through this book, I came to a standstill. It is as if a landslide came down on my path, a debris-filled horizon. That's all I saw.

Many thoughts collided together into a mess, that led to chaos and then very slowly, but surely, to a lack of self-confidence.

I had writer's block.

I've never known what that was before. I never had it. At worst, I would pause for a few minutes, struggling to get my thoughts into words, but never like this. Never for days. Weeks.

I gave myself two months for writing, editing, publishing this book. I want to bring this accomplishment along to my Hawaii vacation in July.

On top of that, I still have my workshops to create. Once I come back from my month-long travels, I must have them setup, begin promoting and preparing myself. These workshops are an extension

60

of my two books. I cannot fully create them without having this second book finished and tied-up with a pretty ribbon.

The extent of responsibility, granted, bitten off by me and no one else, laid on me like a huge weight.

I began to doubt myself, my abilities, and the need for what I had to offer. I began to fear failure. Cloaked within that fear, was an even deeper fear, fear of success!

It wasn't a fear I thought I had, but I did... Success changes lives, people and their environment.

You may gain friends and lose some. You may gain new perspectives and lose the way of life you've always known.

As they say, people prefer the devil they know.

In this case, I decided this devil may not be allowed to stay in my way, so I prayed to God.

I asked, "What is going on, and why? Why am I stuck so suddenly, sunk into my own tracks, going down, inch by inch into the swampy abyss?"

The revelation shook me to the core, I was scared. Paralyzed by my fears. And here I was, preaching fearlessness. Freedom to be true to oneself, etc. I had relapsed into my own dead ways of thinking. I've resurrected doubts, mistrust, disbelief.

And yet, destiny beckoned me. I could see it behind the mist of my own opposition. Behind the fence of thoughts I had allowed into my inner sanctuary. They came quietly. Gently the weeds grew. I barely noticed them and then they grew strong.

I knew I was powerless at that moment. I knew I had to get help from above.

And I did. I prayed. I sought out God. I listened to the words of the prophets.

And finally I obeyed.

I obeyed before, despite huge opposition.

I must digress to share this story but I will, nevertheless, because it is too important a story not to share. Too great of a lesson that I should keep to myself.

As I had mentioned before, my dad was a tough cookie. A tyrant, really. He went through a really dark phase, a patch of history, barren, filled with stumbling blocks.

I know you must be thinking, why is she sharing this dirty laundry? Well, because we all have stories like this. It is not to our shame. To be honest, I must tell the truth. The truth will set you free and not only you, many more like you.

My dad and I clashed, a lot. As the oldest, I was there to protect and stand up for the truth and the preservation of values. It got to the point where I could no longer live in that house, because it was making me physically ill and emotionally unstable. I felt like a puppet, tortured because I was not in control of my own strings.

So I cut the strings and left. (I've carried the guilt of leaving for about two years. I felt like I should've stayed and suffered along with the rest of them.)

To quickly get to the point, one day I was on my knees, by my bed. I was trying to have a conversation with God, it was a rather, silent, quiet moment. Somber, because I knew that the time had come for me to forgive my dad.

I've tried many times before but I couldn't, the anger had consumed me and held me captive. I didn't feel like forgiving him and didn't think I possibly could, but I knew I had to. Why? Because that's what God asks of us.

Look, if God asks something of us, that means it is doable. He will give you all the resources and grace you need.

So, there I was, kneeling, when I realized that the point of being obedient was right here, at the door. I had to open it. So I did.

I didn't know how it was going to be possible, but knew deep in my heart that I had to act then. With disbelief at how I was going to accomplish this, I said, "Alright Lord. You ask me to do this. So I am going to do it. God, I forgive my dad."

As soon as I said those words aloud, a shift happened, a very real sense of a heavy weight rolling off my shoulders. I felt it in the natural, physical, real sense. I actually felt like my body was lighter!

And I realized that the act of obedience had opened the door for grace to come in and perform the work I couldn't do. The anger was gone. I was set free. Finally.

What am I getting at here?

Sometimes, the only thing we can do, no matter how we feel, is to take that first step of obedience, without knowing what happens next.

So that is exactly what I did. I sat down to write, knowing not where to start and asked the Spirit to guide me. And guided I was! I couldn't stop writing. It's almost 3:00 p.m. right now and I've been writing since 8:30 a.m. or so, with intermissions to look after my daughter. And the magical thing is that, today, she slept in and didn't need much of my supervision. She was very happy to play next to me. Being lenient with messes also helps.

I will keep writing until nighttime, setting a promise to myself that I will have my reward after - a hot, steamy bath with books, magazines, tea, and a bit of wine. A girl has to treat herself a little.

I hope that you have learned from this example that all you need to do is be obedient, and God will take care of the rest.

Living a passionate life means to give in to God and to trust Him, on His terms.

Your terms will often fail you because they may be riddled with weeds and shortsighted views.

You can do much better than that. You can let in God to clear out your closets, to straighten your crooked paths and clean up the dirty mess around you.

There is no shame in letting God deal with the No's as well.

Do what you are good at, most of the time

To achieve fast results, you must frequently find yourself in the zone, when time passes by and you feel so fulfilled having done what you just did.

Typically, whatever it is that we enjoy doing so much, with such passion, is something we are really good at.

What are you good at? Find out! It may not be something you are aware of yet!

What is it that you want to be?

I realized that I want to be an Influencer, a Mover and a Shaker, whatever the title is for the person that wants to change the world in a positive way. I want to speak, teach, write and share my message of living a passionate life. It really isn't about me, but about the gifts that are within me. I cannot hide them. I am convinced that the world needs every gift we've got to make it a world we want to pass on to our children.

I am good at inspiring people, motivating, encouraging, and empowering them... in person. I am still learning to do it via other means. But that's ok. I am a work in progress. We all are, so let's be kind to one another.

I am good at writing short pieces, not so yet practiced at writing longer prose, but I am willing to try.

Winners are always willing to try.

I am good at motivating and pushing myself forward, so I try even harder, knowing that I will gain wisdom that I can share with others, so they can have an easier time than I did. Why do I care? Because, I can only make so much of a difference, but a collective can alter the course of our planet.

So I keep trying, because I am willing. And because one day I want to be on Oprah, if she lives long enough.

Of course, you may be good at things that don't bring you joy. As a perfectionist, and a type A personality, I always was good at most things. I knew if others could do it, so could I. If an A was available, I could definitely go after that mark.

Please differentiate between things you are good at and you enjoy, and the other category, things you are good at by force.

We are all innately good at something. A bit of cultivation would bring us closer to perfection, a state of being called - excellence.

You cannot devote all the time you need, to things you are forced to do, to become excellent. Or if you do, it will take so much time and effort, compared to the one that was truly good innately, and passionate about that particular thing.

Save yourself some struggle. This life needs a little ease to it. Find things you are good at, passionate about, find enjoyable and fulfilling.

For example, I am passionate about speaking my mind through a written form.

I can whip out an essay on a topic I enjoy, in 30 - 45 minutes, easy.

I've talked to others who shared with me that it takes them days. A paragraph a day, maybe.

For them it's a struggle. For me it's a self-fulfilling task that brings me immense satisfaction.

From that deduction, I can say that I would probably enjoy being an Author. They probably would enjoy doing something else with their precious time.

You know what I've been loving lately? Something I wasn't sure I would in the days past -making videos where I share my inner thoughts with the world.

At first, I felt super awkward. I was impressed with people that seemed to have so much fun in each video that they created. So liberated. And then, one video at a time, I became hooked.

Another lesson I've learned is that to be really great at whatever it is that you do, you have to be authentic. Yes, painfully authentic. Being truly you will set you apart. It is when you don't want to expose yourself and your true colors that you blend in, in an unexceptional wallflower kind of way.

Showing your true colors is not always a negative phrase. You may have colors that are truly worth sharing. Colors that add depth and beauty to this world.

To be authentic, one must be brave. Why? Being authentic means exposing the vulnerable parts of you. Your heart. Your spirit.

What happens when you do that? You run the risk of being hurt while taking a chance that people may see something in you that they will find valuable and inspirational: a reflection of themselves.

In any relationship, for it to be strong, full of promise and thriving, the parties must be authentic.

I want us, the author and the reader, to learn to trust each other. It will bring us great pleasure to recognize ourselves in one another and to learn to love what we see, bringing us healing within us, because what we see, oftentimes is simply this: a reflection of ourselves.

I hope that at one point we will get so good at being ourselves that it will no longer be a role we are playing, but a life we are living. There is nothing more fearless nor honorable than being the you that God designed you to be.

Don't take anything personally

You've learned to slow down, and now you are speeding up. You are most likely dealing with people on a level you haven't been used to before. That's ok. Give yourself a bit more grace.

I've struggled with expressing myself while explaining to someone what It is that I do, or trying to do, because, quite frankly, I didn't know it myself at that time.

Sometimes, in the action of doing, only then we can find out or learn something about our next move or ourselves.

Don't stop moving because you don't know how to do something. Don't lose momentum. Do the best you can with the knowledge at hand, do some homework, don't be silly, but don't be a slave to perfection.

That's the fun part about this journey to self-fulfillment; you never know what you will encounter! The surprises will blow you away. Opportunities and people that you will encounter, because you just went for it, will be incredible.

Don't live with regrets.

When you are starting out, people may not have faith in you. They may not know you, not care about you or will judge you based on the judgment of their own abilities.

They may exclude you from opportunities where, you feel, you would be a perfect fit. They may not believe in your commitment or passion.

That is not personal. It rarely is. It is based on their view of life, expectations and outcomes.

Remember, they are doing the best they can with whatever information they have at hand.

If they are a business person, they may be trying to do the best they can for their business.

On the other hand, a lot of people will take your decisions personally. It will hurt both of you, but if you want to succeed in life, you will have to learn to make difficult decisions and be committed to staying the course.

Going after new things you've never done will be fraught with vulnerability, indecision and doubt. You may feel excited and shaken at the same time.

Don't allow their No's to be understood as a No to YOU as a person. It doesn't mean that you haven't got it. It just means that they don't see it.

It's hard to persuade someone that lacks vision.

The bookstore that said No to me, didn't say I was a bad writer. They just didn't think it was the right opportunity for them. I can respect that. They are doing the best they can.

The people that didn't want to sell my stuff, they too, were doing the best they could to supply their clients with the items they thought they would prefer best.

It really isn't personal, it's just business.

Don't waste your precious creative force, your energy on feeling emotions that will never serve you. But if you do, do what I do. I transform the negative feedback into a positive experience and a force that fuels my momentum.

I tell myself, "I will show them! They will wish they said yes!"; whatever will help you get through that moment and empowers you.

Or just train your brain to see a challenge as a source of growth. If you say yes to that challenge, you will indeed stretch yourself, and like a torn muscle, you will rebuild, stronger than ever.

This is the perfect time to tell you of my greatest challenge thus far. I've discussed it with friends that have started out on their passionate journeys, be it a business or a platform of influence.

So here it goes. There is such a phenomenon called "we-want-you-to-be-experienced-but-we won't-give-you-any", otherwise known as "too-small-of-a-fish-but-we-won't-feed-you-either".

That will be one of your outer struggles. The environment will require something of you that it is not willing to give you. A whole lot of you will hear rejections based on your lack of experience but no one will give you the chance to catch up on that experience. That's when you need a break from God. I am still waiting for mine.

I don't blame the environment. To be truthful, I may do the same thing. It takes a strong person to recognize someone's greatness and to take a chance on them. They must be on some level, divinely inspired.

Again, it's nothing personal. If you stay consistent, the break will come. If you show a history of persistence and excellence in the sphere of influence you do have, someone will notice.

And then again, I've learned a tough lesson not to depend on men to promote me, to give me a hand. The results are usually not as great as when my help comes from the Lord.

He skips many steps. He is the most decorated chess player in the Universe, because when He makes a move, it's unmistakable. Full of power and precision, that when recognized, tells you that it was only Him, not man.

Don't apologize for your dreams

Don't apologize for the dreams and passions that God placed within you. There is nothing wrong with following through with the goodness in your heart. There is everything wrong in burying your God-given talents and denying what He wants to do through you.

People will always misunderstand your intentions based on what is going on within themselves.

If they aren't honest, then they will see others as dishonest and etc. If they would only do good works for a particular reason, then they will assume your reasons are identical to theirs. People can only see what they've got.

People will tell you that you think you are better than they are. And you may not think so, while being so. There is nothing wrong in recognizing your competence, skill, drive, and passion, which may be greater than someone else's, but the failure to recognize the intrinsic value of every person is what will get you. It will block you from enjoying other people's presence, help, support and advice.

Advice may be free flowing when you start moving along your journey, but be careful to sift the great advice from someone who's been there from the not-so-great advice from someone who knows little and wants to keep you from moving forward. Even if they are truly trying to help you, knowing little, how much can they actually give you?

Please look at the people and the fruit of their lifestyle. You are who and what you surround yourself with. Surround yourself with dreamers and doers and you will be dreaming and doing like never before!

When I was a little girl, I used to dream for hours. I would spend an inordinate amount of time daydreaming on the swings, in my special tree, and in the back of our yard, with my back to the bushes behind me. Surrounded by greenery and away from the prying eyes, I would succumb to the delight of what can be, what will be and what should be.

I would imagine detailed situations. My desire to help others would, most often, result in my imaginations circling around mission's work. As a child, I thought that the best way to help others would be to become a missionary.

Now I believe that the power of the written word can easily overwhelm the world, from wherever I am to wherever you are.

Dreaming was an escape and an opportunity to create, it took me out of what was static and into what was pliable.

Cultivate your unconventional thinking through dreaming. In your imagination, you will find no obstacle, no boundary, and no one else that will tell you that it cannot be done.

Enjoy the freedom to see yourself succeed. Revel in the possibility. Try out various scenarios. I don't care if you feel silly, imagine it as if it already is. Smile. Feel the joy. Let the passion overcome you.

The more frequently you engage in this delightful pastime, the more you will begin to change your thinking. You will start to believe, bit by bit.

Because you will start believing, or wanting, what yousee in your mind's eye, you will start acting on those dreams.

Dreams are the vitamins of life. They strengthen us and attack the free radicals, the disbelief of others. Dreams take our blood to the boiling point, a point from which you cannot be inactive, the energy will have to be expressed.

Whatever gives you life, fills you with joy, excites you, reinvigorates you, is never a waste of time.

See small

Every little thing counts. Everything you do matters. Every feeling you have is not insignificant but has deep reasons for being alive.

There is a reaction for every action. A consequence for everything under the sun, be it good or bad.

A sum of little actions can add up to something quite substantial. As well as a sum of inactions. There is no such thing as being in-between.

Everyone is a believer, in the good or the bad. It is up to you to realize where you stand.

Pay attention to every thought you have, because it is not a dead thought. Thoughts lead to actions. For every action, there is a reaction. What sort of reactions are you experiencing right now? Perhaps it is time to change your thoughts.

If you don't believe that you have what it takes to succeed, then you are believing the opposite. If you don't believe in abundance, then you believe in lack.

You catch my drift.

Pay attention to the least of these, and in this case, it isn't children we are talking about or people of no importance. We are talking about the building blocks of your success.

Focus on your unique abilities, desires and experiences. Allow God to utilize all three to paint a picture of significance and of consequence.

You are a unique expression of God that cannot be minimized. In doing so, we minimize the Creator. Accept your destiny. Let go of the fear of greatness. Cultivate the field that was given to you to bring much fruit!

Cultivate the spirit of excellence

Cultivating the spirit of excellence may be lost on some in the time of when "it's all about me and what can I get out of it".

It is hard to do so especially when you think that no one is looking. And perhaps no one is. Perhaps no one notices what you are doing and no one cares, but for the sake of your integrity and your own personal growth and satisfaction, do try.

It will be worth it in the end.

A time will come when all your unseen dedication and hard work, persistence and heart, will no longer be hidden.

The time will come when the world will take that chance on you and will recognize what you've known all along - you've got something special.

It takes a very special person to keep doing things well in the darkness. But trust me, imagine how well prepared you will be in the light!

A person that develops a character of excellence will always be prepared for the right opportunity. They are the ones that will perform well and will be in high demand. They are the ones that leadership needs to take notice of.

Are they consistent, are they persistent, loyal, truthful? Do they give credit to others when credit is due? I've seen people be afraid to do so because of the fear of being minimized and underscored, but I feel those people who can highlight others should be commended for their bravery and team spirit. Those are the budding leaders.

A spirit of excellence requires commitment. A spirit of excellence requires a consistency of heart. It requires always taking that extra step, walking that extra mile. Searching for fresh opportunities and always giving it your all, even though no one had required it of you.

What sort of person is interested in cultivating this facet of themselves?

A person who knows that they are destined for greatness, be it on a huge scale or a small scale. They have an inner drive to pursue and to receive. To try again and do it better because, yes, it can be done. They enjoy the growth process and see challenges as opportunities for change and making something just a little bit better.

They are not afraid to stretch themselves and if they are, they do it in spite of fear.

That type of person is extraordinary.

What's an ordinary person? A person that forgot how extraordinary he or she is.

By that definition, it may be my own, but I've got no fears of redefining terms, every person has extraordinary capabilities.

Yes, every person. I don't care who you are or who you think you are.

You've got what it takes to do anything you set your own mind to. It may take time. It may take effort.

It will take a lot of heart and a bit of heartache, but you will make a shift in your life and the life of others.

We all want you to be the best version of you. You've got something we all need. You were made to share it with us. You no longer can keep it hidden.

Once you recognize yourself in the words above, and some of you will, right now, the first step to getting there is to start doing things right.

By right, I mean, with all you've got. Bring it and own it.

I used to think only special people can write LinkedIn articles, with years of expertise and schooling, etc.

Guess what? I realized I am an expert as well. I motivate people. I am real. I tell it how it is.

I can no longer be hidden.

Come on a journey with me. Do something that brought you fear. I am not afraid to write anymore, whatever audience it may be, because I know who I am and I am following my dreams.

There will always be opposition and criticism.

There will always be people that sing you praises.

You must always stick to your truth.

And it starts now.

Give your heart to your dreams. Include people that can help you as well. Don't think you can get there alone. You may, but you may not be as quick.

Recognize the potential in others and nurture those sparks. Value the beauty of others.

We are all the same and yet everyone is so unique.

And that's the beauty of God's creative genius.

Be audacious

I wish I could say that I always had the audacity to speak, but I didn't.

We can all blame our upbringing, culture, parents, everything else but ourselves. And that's a valid point. As children, we are indeed shaped by our circumstance. As adults, it is our responsibility to take the little child within ourselves and take them out of that circumstance.

Stop being the victim. In doing so, we become empowered.

How often do you find yourself silent at work? How many times have you passed up an opportunity to share your ideas or your disapproval? How many times have you seen something that just wasn't right, and ignored it because you were afraid to be confrontational or, even, worse, found invalidated?

I wish, looking back, that I had the courage to speak even though I may have meant very little to others, insignificant, because I was so low on the ladder.

I was taught that good girls don't engage in confrontation, that Christians don't "fight back", don't rock the boat, etc., and so I didn't.

So I let some people slide when I shouldn't have. They had seniority and money. I had neither. The fright of being fired held me captive.

My dear, there is power in being financially stable. Save money so you can have something to tide you over in case you do end up speaking up and things turn sour.

Imagine how awesome it would feel to know that you can say your piece and not have to worry about biting your tongue... hard?

We need whistleblowers. We need people of integrity and honor. Of inordinate courage and spirit. I am that person now but I missed so many chances to do the right thing.

If someone questions your audacity to speak, be it known, you have the right as a human being to put integrity and honor before profit and fitting in. You have the right to unburden your soul, and in that way, setting your spirit free.

By not speaking up, we are loading up our soul with boulders, too heavy to carry at times and in that essence, binding our spirit. If we do too much of that, I am sorry, but your spirit will not fly, will not be free to be creative and to let your soul be the best it can be.

The outward struggle is a result of an inner struggle.

To resolve the inner struggle, we most often have to let something go outwardly. It is all connected.

Don't for a minute think that if you don't speak up, that you will not be hurt. In the process of being silent, you are hurting your innermost self.

Most often we keep hurting that little child that we still have within. As an adult now, you have the right to protect that little sweet thing that is you.

There are good times and bad times that ask of us to speak up.

Don't miss the good times, either. Your idea may seem silly because it is so odd, so different, so crazy unusual but it could be just the thing to revolutionize the world.

Your approach can be so audacious, so confrontational to the way things have been done before, but who cares. You can redefine terms and systems. You can create the new norm. Someone did that before you. Why can't you?

Live a little. Be you. Be true. Be Audacious.

Don't minimize yourself in front of others, be authentic

How often have you felt that you cannot speak your truth because others would judge and say that you are either trying too hard, are too lofty or just "too special"?

I've had moments where I had to stifle my answers and my growth in the midst of a crowd.

For example, during one of my playground outings at the Bishop Park, I ran into a bunch of moms. That was the day I finally received my T-shirts from the screen printer. I was so proud!

Feeling emboldened by this accomplishment, I asked the moms if they were willing to have a look at what I've got. Feeling assured by their interest, I went to the Jeep to get the items. As I proceeded to show them my collection, one lady dramatically responded by saying that she is NOT a motivated mama (my T-shirts have that phrase on the backs of them). I so badly wanted to say, " You are right, you aren't. Do you want to know how I know this? Because you are what you think you are!"

But I held my tongue. This could've been a teachable moment but I fell short. I was still a bit intimidated with my growing position in the spotlight.

I laughed her comment off, along with the rest of the group, but that moment will stay with me for life.

Truth is a deciding factor in what separates the norm from the great. Don't try to fit in; otherwise you will be like everyone else. You need to let your own light shine. Be brave.

Having said that, pay attention to the people around you that minimize themselves on a regular basis. Help them see the truth. Help them see their unique value, beauty, and the opportunity that life has for them.

In helping others see the light, we establish the light within ourselves. It is in giving that we find so much more is given back to us.

See BIG

I want you to see the big picture. We get so caught up in the details that it is sometimes hard to see where we've come from and where we are going.

It is amazing to be able to master the minutia of the everyday life, but to find passion in it, one must complement the seeing small with seeing big. It is a very necessary part of the Passion Equation.

If we don't see the big picture, we may become so stuck in seeing small, that we don't raise up our heads to scan the horizon for fresh opportunities or storms coming.

We need to be prepared and aware of the times and the seasons.

You need to have a vision, a destination, something to aim towards. Don't make the big picture, small, to increase the chance of it being attainable. You would be selling out to fear and cutting yourself short.

The way I see it, reach as high as you can, for the sun, and you will get a few stars along the way.

Whenever you get worn out by the details of the day, remind yourself of where you are going, and that in the scheme of things, a day will not make that big of a difference. It is the accumulation of days that will.

If one opportunity didn't pan out, there will be others that will. Don't despair. Raise your head above the clouds.

Keep your eyes on the prize and everything else will line up.

Dormant passion versus expressed passion

A lot of people say that they aren't passionate enough or lack passion altogether.

I feel them, but I cannot sympathize or mourn with them because that wouldn't be necessary. And it isn't true.

We all have the ability to reach greatness, glory, success and self-fulfillment. All of us.

We all have passion. Yes, you, too. If you feel that you don't, then perhaps your passion is hiding somewhere, unexpressed, but nevertheless it is still there. Just because it isn't sunny everyday doesn't mean that we no longer have the sun.

I don't want to cater to the helpless and enable them in their helplessness. It wouldn't serve me nor help them in any long-term way.

All of us need to know that we've got what it takes.

Take me for example. I didn't know the extent of my passion until I allowed it to be expressed and unlocked at the beginning of 2017. It is May now, just five months into my journey and I am now on my second book, part of an amazing group of women, and beginning to notice that I am indeed inspiring others and making a difference in this hungry and thirsty world.

During a UGA Small Business consulting session, the lady behind the desk asked me how my life was as I presumed to be a life coach. Granted, I am still in the process of becoming certified and plan to get it done soon after this book. I think she was surprised when I said that my life was great! I loved it! I could only see it getting better and better.

People may not believe you because everything they see is based on their own judgment of themselves. If she doesn't believe in a great, self-fulfilled life, then she couldn't possibly believe that this was happening to me.

I wasn't upset. I was pretty happy to have shocked her. I love shocking people and catching them off guard.

It's the rebel in me. I remember I was in sixth grade and a girl threw out a few choice words at me, calling me weird. She didn't realize she was paying me the greatest compliment she could. I so hated conformity that she actually made my day! Thank you, bully-girl. I wonder where you are now!

So going back to passion. Now, where were we?

Oh, yes, dormant versus expressed.

Look, we are born with a right to live passionately, to follow our dreams, set goals, become self-actualized and self-realized. Children run around with such freedom of expression! I love watching their enthusiastic faces, filled with life.

Something happens to us during our lifetime - we get frozen, stale, stunted. What gives? We believe someone else's "truth" and disregard what we know is the truth within our hearts. Our parents especially are strong conduits of that message. They are our greatest influence. They think they are doing us a favor by making us do practical things that will set us on a path of being accepted, and like everyone else.

And we stop believing. We stop dreaming.

Not because we wanted to, but because slowly we began to agree with the message that stuck to us like glue. Crazy glue.

With every new dream, we would go through the same process. Stuff it down and deep inside one's consciousness, because it isn't going to happen to me, right? Over and over and over again we did this. Layer and layer upon a crushed dream.

I know, I did this with tremendous regularity.

And finally something happened. It was a realization without fanfare but it broke the damn like a banshee of earthquakes. My world was shaken and I could not hold it in any longer or I would explode. I had a message that screamed out to be heard. What was invisible, now wanted to be visible with an all-consuming force.

I had to learn to speak, to think, and act with freedom. At times I went overboard because that level of self-expression was very new and rare to me.

My husband would be upset and take things personally because he thought something was wrong with me, I wasn't myself. That perhaps I wasn't satisfied with life because I wasn't satisfied with him. Men always try to solve a problem and not just appreciate things for what they are; simple, messy moments of life that will get sorted out eventually.

There came a point, after opening the door to my inner self, that an avalanche of tired dreams woke up and stormed out of the holding.

They ran all over me. Crushing me under their presumptuous weight.

I had to give in, to surrender. I couldn't fight. I would be outnumbered one to one thousand.

I've had such an accumulation of dormant passion that when it dared to come out and become expressed, I didn't know how to handle all that momentum.

I was like a newborn deer learning to walk anew. I had to trust that one day I would be like a free gazelle, jumping, comfortable in my own new prance.

Ok, so perhaps you believe me that you have dormant passions residing within you. Thank you and that's great. You are on your way to something much more powerful than you are. Belief.

Being able to believe is a very powerful creative force. Nothing can stand in the way of faith.

The simple act of believing that you have passion within you already, will give it the will to live again, to appear in ways that are small and then on levels unprecedented.

Even the act of willing to believe will have the power to shift the environment for you.

Hey, start small, build a foundation first, if that makes you happy. Or be like me, running at full blast, running with my dreams, propelled by my passion and zest for self-expression within my now attainable goals.

I am so convinced that it will happen for me that I can literally taste the culmination of my desires.

Expressed passion is the fuel that gives us life and the ability to pursue our dreams on another level. Fuel that fire, woman. Fuel that life.

You are so beautiful and wonderfully made, so precious to God, that you cannot deny Him your true self any longer. You are His masterpiece, a divine creation of His passion, imagination and love. An imprint of God is written all over you. You cannot fail.

Take the reserves that you've accumulated and spread them all over your coming days.

You are not alone

You are not alone. There have been so many wonder-filled examples of lives well-lived by women that came before you.

There will be many more after you and there are currently enough residing in this time and space alongside you.

You are not unique in the sense that no one can ever understand what you are going through. Ergo, don't fatten up your excuses because you feel justified in your solitary experience.

That is not true. There are plenty of motivated moms out there that had to adjust their lifestyles and give up many Netflix sessions so they could finish up work and accomplish a goal. They had to give up time with their friends, drinking coffee and running in the park with their kids.

How did they do it? They kept their eyes on the prize. They knew that temporary sacrifices will lead to permanent change and long-lasting legacy of strength and influence. They knew that each moment they persisted was a moment well spent.

They took care of themselves the best way they knew how because having enough fuel in their tank was important. They couldn't become self-sacrificing to an unhealthy state. They had to make sure they were breathing before they could take care of someone else.

May I suggest that you surround yourself with like-minded individuals, ladies that are equally passionate about their lives and that face similar challenges? Doing so, you will learn so much about where the future is headed, as you share ideas, concepts, and the creative genius that resides within you.

You will enjoy being part of a supportive community. Create a Facebook group or similar, where you can easily keep tabs on each other and send out support at the proper time. Hold each other accountable for following through on the steps you've committed to. Celebrate each other's successes. Believe in one another.

Women need to hold hands and rise up together. It is time to make a difference to the future lives of our own daughters and granddaughters. We are responsible for making this happen.

Cultivate your child-like curiosity

Be curious about everything. Learn about the wonders of this world, the human race and the heavens. See yourself within the greatness of God. Seethe big picture. Whatever you do may make a huge impact but at the same time, no matter what you do will change the course of this planet or the wind patterns or the layout of the mountains. People will continue living and animals will continue roaming this world.

What I am trying to say here is this; don't be afraid to look like a fool or make mistakes, to fail and fall flat on your face. That's part of the process! Embrace the process! Embrace the failures of past ventures. That's where they will be, in the past! Glean a valuable lesson and move on, wiser and stronger, and more effective than ever before.

Keep learning constantly. Don't be intimidated by the material. Currently, I need to learn how to code and work my website with google analytics and lots of other froufrou terms. It's not something I am comfortable with but, I know that once I master these scary concepts, I will feel like a winner that scaled the Mount Everest, victorious!

Take every challenge with hope, positivity, optimism, and joy because you are on your way to a better you. Every challenge has the tremendous capacity to set you up with incredible opportunities for growth and the means to tap into your potential.

In the process, you will learn that some of the things that scared you are precisely the things you are good at! Allow yourself to be pleasantly surprised!

I am becoming much better at putting myself out there to be seen, noticed, discussed and appreciated.

I am learning to speak my mind and to say the truth, although that is not easy. Truth isn't always pretty. It is not often palatable, although very necessary.

Go out there and explore your world. Get out of your comfort zone and talk to the people. Friend someone new on Facebook. Engage in conversations on social media.

I never thought I would like Twitter, hated it even at one point, but now I am developing a craving for it.

The cork that stopped my speech is no longer there. The words just tumble out of me, at times with a sweet melody or a bubbly beat, and at other times, tone-deaf and haphazard, but that's ok. I am still learning and will continuously learn through life.

What matters is not the mistakes we make but how we improve over time. If you can see your progress and notice the changes in your behavior, you've got something great going on.

It is ok to stumble like a kid, pick yourself up, smile and move forward.

The one characteristic I so thoroughly admire about children is their fearlessness within their creative process. They believe that their pictures are beautiful, their play dough statues are worth mentioning, and that the macaroni necklaces are super classy on their mama's neck.

Allow yourself the nonjudgmental space to be creative.

You may have accused yourself of not having a creative bone in your body but that accusation nests far from the truth.

Everyone I've met so far has the potential to be creative or thrive creatively on a very high level.

Ok, so why have you not seen that about you?

Either you are blinded and have taken your ability for granted, or because, unfortunately, you just simply aren't in the environment that would let you blossom.

For seven years of my life I worked at a company where I just didn't fit in. I was amidst engineers who talked shop. Who seemed smart. I couldn't converse much about their gadgets, machinery, or product. Because of this inability, I was perceived as less capable than they were.

I would frequently think that of myself as well.

I couldn't often be noticeably creative, because what creative moments I had weren't paid attention to, not because they were not appreciating them, but because they simply weren't seeing them.

You see, I didn't speak their language.

How often I've seen immigrants be deemed stupid because of the language barrier!

How often they've felt stupid and accepted that thought and made it their own!

Times changed. I moved.

I am now in an environment, propelled by the special burst of courage and energy, received through my daughter's birth, where suddenly I feel like I get it. I do and say things that are understood and welcomed. I realized that I am quite fluent!

Because of that increase in confidence and belief in self-worth, I started to break down my creativity barriers. I realized that the only true barrier was my own self. My deep-seated, deep-rooted beliefs.

What am I saying? It may not be you, it may truly be the environment.

If you cannot change jobs or move, find opportunities or hobbies that you enjoy. Surround yourself with people that "get it" and whom you "get" also.

The stronger you become in standing your ground of self-worth, and validated by your own beliefs about yourself, the more freedom you will have to express yourself on all levels.

Creativity begets creativity.

Start somewhere. Just start. Not tomorrow. Today.

Although I constantly harp on this one point, I do it with specific reason, to remind you and drill it down into your subconscious; you cannot deny the world your true self.

We are losing out because of your fears that come from wrong beliefs.

It's time to turn to the new page.

Spring is so fresh with promise.

Your day today is filled with promise.

You are our promise.

A promise that our future has hope.

A promise that our future has a future.

Don't bend under that weight.

Thrive.

Dare to risk it all

Pursuing your dreams requires so very much! It requires that you give everything you've got. For some people it means risking ridicule, judgment and loss of self-worth. Going after something you want with passion, full throttle, will expose your vulnerabilities like never before. You will be raw, bleeding at times but you will have to continue. The results will be worth it.

You will make so many mistakes that you may become convinced that no one else is going through this but you.

I've made far too many mistakes to count. Far too frequently, and most often, with tremendous gumption. At times, I haven't seen past my own nose and fixated on one idea, I've missed other vantages, opportunities, and points of view.

I've written emails I've later regretted. I've made friends with people I shouldn't have. I've persuaded people to join me when the timing wasn't right. I've hurt people when they couldn't keep up with my fervent pace.

Some find me abrasive, too passionate, too driven, too intimidating.

I could've held my tongue and promised less. Spoke up when I should have and not missed the opportunity to act and make things just a little bit better.

Anyway, you get the picture. There are lots of should've's and could've's. Lots of misplaced idealist notions and rightly interjected views that were quiet honestly, misunderstood.

We all make mistakes. I made plenty.

What I've learned is that a successful person responds to mistakes differently. Immediately, I look at the things I've done right. I start looking at the bigger picture, reminding myself that this is not a stacking game, my dreams will not come crushing down. Looking back at the history of my accomplishments boosts my spirits, and I can kindly forgive myself for making an error, especially if it were a result of a learning curve.

Please understand, if you are new to something, you WILL, inevitably, make a million mistakes. The greater the dream, the more mistakes you will probably make between the many steps you will have to take. You will slip and slide on that ladder. The point is to stay on it and to continue moving forward.

Give yourself permission to make mistakes. At times, the more mistakes you make, the better you become, a sign that you've tried so many new things. That's called bravery, my friend.

We all get embarrassed. It's an unfortunate human trait, or perhaps fortunate, because it assists our conscience. Anyway, it is never fun to be deeply humiliated by someone over an oversight, especially if they aren't very kind to us. At moments like this, give yourself a lot of grace. Go have some fun, treat yourself, make yourself feel better. Invest in making yourself feel good, fill your reserves of strength in preparation for a wonderful comeback. What doesn't kill you, makes you stronger. If you take this incident on board, as a lesson learned, it will only add to your personality and capability.

Don't be ashamed of asking for help, by the way. A good leader will recognize that you ask because you actually care about getting the job done right.

Don't be so intimidated by making a mistake that you avoid taking chances, risking. You will never be great if you continue to do the same old thing. One definition of insanity may as well be: to expect great things by doing ordinary things.

I've seen so many people tremble, frightened to be chastised by the boss and by the community at large. They avoid standing out and instead prefer to bask in the shadows, wallflowers. They'd rather pace through life, barely noticed, barely making a dent to accommodate their great need for self-preservation. And that is ok for some, but if you aspire to make a stand, to be a leader, that path of least resistance is not for you.

If you take the path least traveled, you will have lots of mountains and jungle to overcome. In the midst of this friction and learning, sparks will fly, indeed.

At times, you can't control where they land, and some things may get singed. Fact of life, success is never a smooth sailing. It is a lot of hard work, day in and day out. Year in and year out. You get the picture.

So, having said all of that, what I want you to internalize is this: You are amazing. You are already going after your dreams vigorously. You are doing the right things. You are consistent. Be proud of how far you've come. Don't make it any harder on yourself by focusing on your mistakes. Celebrate all of your successes! Don't waste your energy. Move on to something more productive. I am sure that next time you will not make that mistake again. Hey, there's progress. That's awesome.

We are all human. When someone makes a mistake, give them some grace. Help them save their face. It will only make you look better.

Follow your dreams. Live your life to the fullest. Be kind. Be good.

Extend the helping hand.

And next time you make a mistake, don't make an elephant out of a fly. Swat it away.

And then you keep moving forward.

We are a work in progress. Honor yourself in that progress.

Honor others as well.

If you view everything as a learning moment, you will find the means to utilize your lessons in such a way that they will bring you even greater glory.

Be careful to write off a mistake as a mistake. It could become a huge missed opportunity.

The more I appreciate what is around me, happening to me and within me, the more I can enjoy life and see my opportunities. I find it interesting that the more we acknowledge our progress and take pride in what was accomplished, the more empowered we become by our very own selves.

It is no crime to inspire and empower oneself. There is no crime in finding joy in little or big-ticket items or events. Joy is joy. Sometimes little joys, combined, overpower something much greater than any one of them.

Look at how far you've come. While reading this book, you are undoubtedly somehow changed and a bit further along on your own path to success. Love your story. Cherish your moments of growth, progress, and delight in who you are; a magical human being with unlimited potential. That is something to be grateful for.

I am thankful for my story. It had pitfalls, but mostly blessings. Pitfalls were surely blessings in disguise. I couldn't see the large-scale picture, so it was easy to get mired in the heavy details.

There is still so much left. This is only the very tip of the iceberg, the blink in my beginning.

I feel like so much has changed, as if I am living another life. And that is true. So much did change and I am indeed living a different life. A life I could only dream of. And now, it is unfolding gently into a reality that inspires me every single day to continue to thrive, to believe, and to share with others the gems of wisdom that I've picked up along the way.

There is more to come

At times, the frustration of getting nowhere is so absurdly strong that we cower at the intense feelings we may have. Rather than process those feelings, we quit, while we are still intact, not realizing that every process of shattering and rebuilding will only make us stronger, more resilient, and more beautiful.

The process of growth is never easy and no one said it would ever be easy. Life may not be fair but what is fairly accurate is that a winner never quits and a quitter never wins.

Therefore, I've decided to eradicate the option to quit.

I will never quit. That word is not in my dictionary.

At the beginning of this year, a new phase has been unlocked for me. I realized that I am no less than anyone else and having accepted this truth, I concluded that if wonderful things happen to others, then they can also happen to me.

Each morning I would wake up determined to create change, to go after my dreams.

I knew that consistency would get me there. It wasn't a question of will it; it was a question of when. Being a mommy entrepreneur, author and motivator, it is never a breeze finding the time to do anything for myself, period (my kid is jumping on my back as we speak). I had to make up my mind to use my time wisely. Whatever free time I had to myself would now have to be allocated to working on my dreams and goals, day in and day out.

Repetitive work but also fulfilling... The great secret about following your dreams is that you are going after something you are meant to do, meaning that most of your actions taken towards getting "there" will be a labor of love. You will enjoy your growing process, your newfound talents and expressive creativity.

The not so great truth is that your path will no doubt be littered with obstacles.

You will hear many No's. You will hear gazillion excuses from others and yourself. Many will not understand why you do what you do, or set out to do.

Some will think you are too self-righteous, too intimidating, or just simply too much.

I've had all those terms thrown my way. That "too much" that they see in me is a vibrant flame of passion that fires me up and burns all opposition. It adds zest to my life and a pep to my step.

There is nothing wrong with caring too much, too deeply or too passionately. We all need people that can get the job done, that can shake up this world and change the spiritual trajectory of this planet.

The ordinary person will never be able to do that. But what is an ordinary person?

A person that forgot how extraordinary he or she is. So not all is lost.

You are a person who has what it takes. How do I know that? Because you have passion.

Before you stop me right there, let me remind you. Yes, we all have passion, be it dormant or expressed, we all have this mysterious ability. It's just a question of waking it up!

Now, let's put together some of the concepts you've read about, up to this point, into a mini program.

Here are the three tips that have worked for me. Once you accept them and make them your own, your life will have no choice but to adjust and steer its course in a more positive direction.

Dreams do come true. You CAN reach your goals.

Each time I hear a No, I have learned to re-program my brain to receive it as a positive comment. I've told myself that with every No, I will only grow stronger. The people that have overlooked me yesterday will no longer be able to overlook me tomorrow. The first tip is to frequently stir up this affirmation: With every No, I will only get stronger.

Here is the second precious tip. I see myself as the one that has already achieved her dreams and goals. I visualize myself as having already arrived. The ability to do that helps me to not be attached to people and circumstance as my way of "getting there". I don't take it personally when people say Yes, and then soon enough they say No. Trust me. I've had plenty of those.

And guess what? It's not you. It really is them. It's nothing personal.

The third tip is a fabulous lesson I've learned that set me free to be me and to keep me moving forward. This is the key lesson that completely eradicated my victim mentality and propensity to quit. I will be forever grateful to the challenges and the emotional anguish that led me up to this moment of epiphany; behind every setback is a setup.

This idea sets you up to use all of your remaining energy not looking at the problem but looking at the solution. All of a sudden you are in charge, you are not a victim, but a productively victorious creation.

This works for me every time. Maybe not exactly at that instant, but it will always come to pass. Trust me, you will look back and realize that most of your moments of greatness and opportunities were a result of a mishap, or what you had perceived as a mishap.

Now that you are no longer afraid of the dreaded No, can see yourself as having achieved it all already, and free to look for the setups in every setback, you no longer need the word quit.

Why? Because you will never use it. Therefore, just lose it.

I can feel and taste what is to come.Because I was not derailed nor crushed by any No's, due to my firm belief and trust that behind every setback is a setup, I constantly scan the horizon for opportunities. It has become a habit. I expect them to come.

For example, although I may have been rejected by a local bookstore in Athens, I was very welcomed by another bookstore, The Front Porch Bookstore, that enjoys selling local authors' work. Bless the Marigold Festival in Winterville! Now I realize, that perhaps, I can start with the surrounding areas first and build up my market to the point where the other local stores will want to carry my work, beg me to be a part of their team. A girl can dream! And dreaming is fun because dreams do come true. Perhaps it will take time and hard work but I am willing, so I bet, you are as well.

I am super excited to start working on a series of workshops or classes for a local wellness center. That will be a wonderful experience in public speaking and getting my message across.

I am constantly trying new things! My message gives me so much freedom to try new things because there are a myriad of ways to inspire, empower, encourage and engage the mommies.

I've started a Maternal Movement YouTube channel to get out there, to engage the online community in a very raw and vulnerable form. It was frightening at first, but now I am getting the hang of things and starting to really enjoy speaking out and being the center of attention. Not that this feeling is new to me. At times I crave it, not in an unhealthy way. I think I am made for this.

One of the very new projects I am working on now is the playlist of videos called Keeping It Real with Nikki and Olga on the Maternal Movement YouTube channel. She is a fellow mama that almost had a heart attack doing the first video but came out such a natural! She makes me proud.

Our kiddos ran us ragged that day. We were on the brink of a meltdown but we stuck through it. Finally, we got everyone in the car, after many failed attempts at even starting the video. In the car, we could control where the kids would go, and even then, if you watch that first video, it was a bit of a controlled mess, but we did it.

We will never let anything get in the way of our message. And that is why I am such a believer in the ladies around me and the ladies around the world, because there are so many moms out there like us, wanting to fight for their dreams, crushing the obstacles, leaving a strong message and a powerful legacy to their beloved children.

I will never stop writing because I believe in the power of the written word. Written word changed my life and it will change yours. It has led me to collaborate with other amazing individuals and to guest write for their platforms. It is amazing to recognize like-minded individuals and to realize that you are not alone.

You will not be left unchanged after reading of this book, I can guarantee you that. If you are not convinced, write to me a month after you read this book. See at first if the seeds of greatness don't germinate within you.

You are made for wonderful, powerful and great things. Are you going to let fear stand in your way? No, you won't.

But what you will start doing right now is believing, believing that things can change, that you and your family deserve better, that you have a valuable message within you and if that resonates with you, go for that first step immediately. Whatever it is, just do something. Look in the direction of your dream. It is there for your taking.

You are a winner. How do I know that? Because you are a mother. Being a mother is the hardest and the greatest job in the world. If you can scale that mountain, you can scale anything. If you feel that you lack inspiration, go and have a real deep look at your child.

Is there not enough inspiration in her eyes? In his laugh? In their innocent touch?

You have everything you need to start now.

You are just a step away from the best of your life!

It is easy to be intimidated by the responsibility of a better tomorrow. You haven't been there yet, but you know that much more will be required of you. You haven't seen it yet, but there's a longing in your heart that seeks that promise, that hope that things will not always be the way they are now.

It is easy to find comfort in the ditch of today's and yesterday's, not because you are satisfied with where you are, but because of the fear that growth will bring more pain, more labor and more than you can possibly give.

Now, let me stop right here, before I completely put you off from reaching higher.

Don't worry about having the ability to "make it" when you embark on this vulnerable and often, lonely, journey. It is but a journey, consisting of many smaller journeys and destinations, and eventually it will bring you somewhere you always wanted to be.

There is a little secret, all journeys consist of steps. Small steps. A step at a time. With each step you will stretch enough, grow enough, to accommodate that step. Don't be overwhelmed by looking at an expansion of time that consists of one hundred steps, just look at one.

Simple. Easy. Just one.

What can you do today to bring you closer to your destination?

What can you do tomorrow?

Each day, focus on that one step at a time. Once you learn how to walk, perhaps then you can run!

We don't expect babies to be talking and walking at the ability of an adult. You shouldn't expect the same.

Now, when you start walking, you will be super tempted to start comparing yourself to others moving along a similar journey. Stop right there. If that type of comparison doesn't inspire you or provides mentorship, don't go down that draining route.

I want you to know that everyone you see has struggled to be consistent with that each one step. Everyone had to put in the work. Perhaps now they are running but you aren't... yet. And that's OK. Everyone has their own pace, too.

No one is more special than anyone else. We all start off the same. We must make a choice to stay put or move forward. Everyone has that choice, no matter the background. Let's not play the victim here, because you aren't one. You are a victorious creation of God. Now play that part.

So today, write out your vision for your life. Don't panic, it may change! You aren't going to be married to that vision forever. Take that as your first step.

What is it that you want? Answer that question to clarify what you are aiming for.

Why do you want it? Answer this one and find your motivator. Whip it out whenever you start feeling sluggish.

The rest of the questions and answers will follow, soon enough, but figure out these two at the onset of your journey.

Throw a party if you want to, get a few people to join you in creating a vision board, plan, etc. The more the merrier. Create an accountability group where you can fuel each other's passion. But you must recognize that, ultimately, the future is in your hands only.

How you make that first move is up to you. How you respond to a countermove is up to you, too. The beauty is in the eye of the beholder.

Do take that first step. You never know what will be behind that door. You may be pleasantly surprised.

Take the word failure and quit out of your dictionary. Those words are useless. They truly bring no use to life. So, if you aren't using them, start losing them.

Once you take that first step, learn to enjoy the journey! Learn to thrive and grow and keep moving forward. You've got this. You've got what it takes.

Don't regret not taking that step. That step may cost you not only the rest of your life, but also the best of your life.

Retreat is not an option.

Nor is defeat.

My birth story

The birth of my daughter has changed the trajectory of my life. It is no longer all about me. I am constantly driven by the need to leave a legacy that will propel her even further into the lands that must be chartered and successes that must be owned.

Because of her existence, I am the way I am now. Each day I become a more compassionate and understanding person, towards others and my own self. I would be remiss to not include the story of my daughter's birth because if it weren't for this experience, I would not be as strong, as powerful, and as multifaceted. I would not know the meaning of passionate living the way I do now.

Here is the account of that awesome experience, written down a few months after her birth, sometime in October of 2015. I've shared this epistle with many future mamas on various occasions.

I would like to share it with you as well.

Victory Epistle: A Birth Story

Dear Lady Warrior:

This is a message about victory and power that comes through bringing a life into this world. It is a message about letting go of control and finding peace in the imperfection that is Birth. This is a vision about an emergence of a woman that is strong, passionate, and inspired to take her experience and to transform it into the rocket fuel that will propel her into heights unseen, untested, but thoroughly attainable because she is fearless.

YOU can do this. How do I know? Because I did it. And if I did it, so can you.

August 11th, 2015

I wake up approximately 1-2 hours before my water breaks. I cannot sleep. I wonder and run through my mind to test and see if I have any stresses that keep me awake, but I find no undue stress. So, I just lie there, experiencing a few cramps, nothing neither frequent nor serious. This is what Braxton Hicks are, I thought. Eventually I decide to get up and visit the restroom.

As I make my attempt to maneuver myself out of the bed, I feel something flow out... and as soon as I finally stand up, the rest just gushes out. My water broke.

5:45 a.m.

Oh my God. I was so unprepared even though I've read countless accounts and listened to tens of proud mamas. Today was the day I was going to write up my birth plan, pack my bag and cast the mold of my belly.

My soul knew and kept me awake. I was high on expectation without even knowing it. Trust the process, lady!

I reach out to Chris, my husband, and wake him with a dazed voice...

"Chris, my water just broke."

"Are you sure you didn't pee yourself?" was his sleepy reply, after which we both jumped into action.

I recalled that a few days ago I was talking to my baby and a strange, very esoteric thought came powerfully through my mind. My baby told me, "Mommy, just wait a little more. I am coming soon." I thought it was my imagination as I had two more weeks to go.

I let my doula know, and right after that notification, I called my parents in Massachusetts to tell them the glorious news that their granddaughter was going to be born that day.

I was shaking and shaking and couldn't stop shaking. Chris tried to be helpful but my body was not my own. I ran to the computer to type up the birth plan, hoping that this would help me calm down.

I had a vision of exactly what my birthing experience would be. I am the quintessential type A personality, the teachers' pet. The one that always sat in the front row, smack dab in the center. I even had a plan for how long it was going to take. Yep, my labor was going to be super comfortable and smooth and would last exactly 8 hours. Precisely. I would labor at home until the last moment and as soon as I was about to pop out the baby, I would run to the hospital on the winds of reason and successful planning and deliver in a seamless execution. I was going to be an example of all that had been done "right".

Thankfully, I didn't know that having my water leave me in such a copious amount meant that I didn't have that layer of protection for me and my baby during the contractions. Labor barely started and something already went wrong.

I typed up the birth plan, printed off three copies. One for us, one for the midwives and one extra, in case someone misplaces one.

My doula arrives and I escort her into the guest room. She tells me to rest but I tell her I will do that as soon as I pack the bags, and basically ask her to stay out of my way until I need her. Feeling pretty in control, Chris and I pack the bags.

I rest. We all watch movies. I walk the perimeter of my yard with dogs for company. As I walk, I go deeper and deeper into myself. The day sets behind the horizon... My doula and Chris come out to join me and sip beer. It was a long day. My contractions were still far apart but getting stronger. I started to lose track of time. I sensed the baby wasn't coming that day.

I remained calm as I listened to the hypnobirthing CDs. I breathed and still felt in control. Chris and I worked on the belly cast to pass the time.

My doula put the Tens unit on my back to help with the pain. It helped and I eagerly pressed the button whenever I sensed a wave coming upon me. Eventually, my doula suggested I get into the tub. I was afraid that the pain control would not be as great in the water as it was with the Tens unit. To my surprise, the water felt amazing!

August 12, 2015

In the wee hours that Wednesday, my doula and I felt that the baby was coming! I was so excited and we contemplated remaining at home to deliver, but finally decided to go to the hospital as we still would've had to make that trip after the birth of the baby.

We raced to the hospital. I tried to breathe through the contractions as I felt every bump in the road. Baby was coming. My suffering was almost over. I was glad, as I was always told that my pain threshold was very low and that I was nuts to do it naturally. I wanted to show it to the doubters. Look at my prowess!

I was firm in my resolve to give birth naturally.

As we walk up to the emergency entrance, at the door we meet a young lady leaning against the wall, who asks me if I am there to give birth. She suggests I get an epidural and then I would feel nothing.

I proudly tell her that no, I was there to do this naturally. NO epidurals!

I recall walking up to the birthing section, stopping to breathe and survive through the contractions... I couldn't reply, I couldn't pay attention to anything around me as I had to go deep within myself to make it through. If anyone talked to me... or near me... I felt sick. I couldn't handle any additional stimulation.

We walked into the room around 2:00 a.m. that Wednesday morning.

After that... time blurred. We expected the baby very shortly as all the signs were there, but she still wouldn't come. I walked the halls. I danced. Listened to CDs over and over. I did my squats and various other formations. The bath was my preferred method as my doula and Chris took turns to pour water over me... for hours. The contractions raced through my body in a ceaseless, merciless wave after wave...

I was hot and cold... I couldn't find comfort in the pools of laboring sweat... The Tens unit had long ago lost its effectiveness in the fight against pain.

Surely this was the time, finally, for the baby to come... It was late evening...

My family was extremely worried... two days passed and no baby.

I stuck to my resolve. I WAS going to do this naturally.

I remember leaning against Chris and silently crying against his chest, two or three times... telling him I couldn't do it anymore. I couldn't go on.

My doula, who had an extensive amount of experience with hundreds of births, many of them high-risk, prepared me for the pushing phase as surely this was the transition time.

We allowed the midwives to check on me as we avoided any checks prior due to the risk of infection as it was so long since my water broke.

I longed eagerly to hear the confirmation of that impeding phase...

I almost died when they told me that I was dilated only 5 cm. I was very soft and the baby was low but I just wasn't opening up. I remember almost crawling up the wall in that bathroom. I contemplated asking for pain relief or a C-section, but I was far from being coherent or able to process and then verbalize any thought.

I felt God left me. I was so sure He was going to bless me as a child of God. I trusted Him. After two days of intense anticipation, I was still only halfway there.

I told Chris to let my family know that I needed their prayers now more than ever as I tried to hold on... one contraction at a time.

The midwives urged us to speed up the process. They brought out breast pumps, dusted them off from a forgotten corner. Repeatedly, they kept pumping me to stimulate the contractions to get stronger... fifteen minutes at a time was the prescribed formula as they didn't want to over stress the body.

I began feeling the prayers as I started recalling various powerful scriptures from the Bible. I was holding on with every last atom of hope and trust as I repeated those verses over and over and over...

I can do all things through Christ who strengthens me.

Nothing is impossible with God.

I remember either falling asleep or passing out between contractions as I went away to a muted someplace and came back into each contraction. I couldn't think past that one contraction. To live, as I felt I was dying, I had to focus on the intensity of the present moment. I would collapse under the thought of more future contractions coming my way.

I remember thinking, this is it for me. I cannot go on. I will expire.

Soon after thinking those thoughts, I heard the voice of my daughter again... in a very mysterious fashion crossing my mind.

She said, "Mommy, I am very sorry. So sorry. I am coming very soon. Just hold on a little more."

I told her as I cried silently, "Take all the time you need, baby. Mommy is all right."

We were a team. Throughout all the frequent checks and monitoring, her heart was strong. She reacted to the contractions like a Lioness - with vigor.

August 13, 2015

I felt fear overwhelm me at one point... Fear of complete lack of control. I didn't know what was coming next and I was scared. So scared.

It was almost a spiritual realization. It was a helpless, cowering sensation as I was turned into water, a form which could take any shape in any container of a circumstance.

I finally felt the overwhelming desire to push at 8 cm. It wasn't something I could control. To try and stop this feeling was like trying to stop a train with your hands, in the middle of the tracks. I had neither energy nor stamina left to attempt.

The midwife team surrounded me in those last hours of my marathon journey. I remember someone urging me not to push but I was helpless in the clenches of this passion. My body writhed and I couldn't stop it. The fire spread in my nether regions as my baby's head finally peeked through. I felt her hair and my spirit was renewed. I was finally, truly, near to my joy.

I was led into the bed for my final pushes. At that final push, I felt that not only did I give birth to my baby but that I also gave birth to myself, a new me... a new era at 2:07 a.m. that glorious Thursday morning.

My baby breathed her first breaths as I cried out over and over-"My baby! My baby! My baby!"

My joy and triumph was palpable and I tasted it and drowned in that sensation. I held my baby as she suckled at my proud breast.

Through the stitching and the uterus being massaged after the birth, I held onto my baby and my Victory.

I knew at that moment that we were one, my baby and I... one team. We can go through anything and surpass any expectation. I felt that I could conquer the world... Like an Amazonian princess on top of the mountain. I felt that the elements and nature would be subject to me!

As the days passed, I started to revisit my birthing experience, processing it one bit at a time. Talking to medics and mothers. I had a lot to process, revisit - chew over and over.

But the conclusion is this:

I found peace in my experience and had forgiven myself and others for not having it my way. I no longer measure my success by my lack of failure. What I called failure, I now call resilience.

I am water now, able to flow. I am unbreakable, now that I was broken.

What a great start to our journey together, my Maya Sophia and I.

We did it. That confidence would carry me through my first days and months of motherhood... sleepless nights and worried mornings, hazy days, and tired afternoons. I knew that I would take each hour, one at a time... as I took hold of my contractions, one at a time.

I feel that my roar is now real, able to flex its muscle, primed to change the world... as in fact, I had changed the world already by giving birth to my baby. It is forever changed; the future had been forever altered because I gave life.

You will never feel as powerful and proudly amazed at yourself as during those first moments of being a mother. Nothing will ever compare to what you just had done. Nothing. Every accomplishment will pale in comparison. You will feel that you haven't lived up to this moment... not truly. Not fully. I promise you that it will all be worth it!

You will be like Chris and I, walking around the shops, restaurants, and cafes, with chests thrice their size, silly grins on our faces. Loopy on love for our baby. The aura of the newborn is huge, consuming everything in its stretch.

And yes, I do want another baby.

Sincerely Yours,

Olga Pyshnyak-Lawrence
Fellow Mother in Arms

Made in the USA
San Bernardino, CA
12 October 2017